Psychology for Teachers

Psychology for Teachers

An alternative approach

Phillida Salmon

Hutchinson
London Melbourne Auckland Johannesburg

Hutchinson Education

An imprint of Century Hutchinson Ltd

62–65 Chandos Place, London WC2N 4NW

Century Hutchinson Australia Pty Ltd
PO Box 496, 16–22 Church Street, Hawthorn,
Victoria 3122, Australia

Century Hutchinson New Zealand Ltd
PO Box 40–086, Glenfield, Auckland 10,
New Zealand

Century Hutchinson South Africa (Pty) Ltd
PO Box 337, Berglvei 2012, South Africa

First published 1988

Set in 11/12 pt Bembo Roman by Input Typesetting Ltd, London

Printed and bound in Great Britain by
Richard Clay Ltd, Bungay, Suffolk

British Library Cataloguing in Publication Data

Salmon, Phillida
  Psychology for teachers: an alternative
  approach.
  1. Educational psychology
  I. Title
  370.15   LB1051

ISBN 0 09 172950 5

In memory of Don Bannister

Contents

Acknowledgements

In the course of writing this book, I have come to be grateful to many people. Mary Baur, Phil Cohen and Jenny Edwards all made encouraging and helpful comments. It proved highly stimulating to work on Kellyan ideas with Lois Graessle and a group of ILEA advisory teachers. David Smail provided a uniquely sensitive and thoughtful sounding-board. Shyama Iyer typed the manuscript with sympathy as well as skill. Noel Byass gave characteristic support.

The author and publishers would like to thank the copyright holders below for their kind permission to reproduce the following material:

Penguin Books Ltd for extracts from D. Barnes, J. Britton, H. Rosen and the London Association for the Teaching of English, *Language, Learner and the School* (Penguin 1969, 1971) © D. Barnes, J. Britton, H. Rosen and LATE, 1969, 1971.
Routledge and Kegan Paul for extracts from Salmon and Claire, *Classroom Collaboration* (Routledge and Kegan Paul 1984).

Introduction

Can there be a case for yet another book on the psychology of education? With the mountain of such books already in existence, have psychologists really anything new to say? Among the many approaches brought to bear on questions of learning and teaching, the voice of George Kelly has scarcely been heard. Yet his ideas seem, more than most kinds of psychology, to speak directly to teachers.

When, in 1955, Kelly first set out his own distinctive psychological approach, he labelled it *personal construct theory*.[1]* This title announced the central importance he gave to the idea that each of us creates our own reality, that we can know the whole world we live in only through the personal interpretations, or constructions, that we make of it. At a period when a basically mechanistic approach was dominant in psychology, this theory offered a radically new departure. In complete contrast with the assumption that people are to be explained by externals – their histories, their circumstances – Kelly insisted that human beings can be understood only by reference to their inner realities – their systems of personal constructs.

For all its imaginative potential, and the escape it offered from the narrowness and dreariness of mechanistic explanations, personal construct psychology[2] might have remained an obscure academic byway. That it did not was due to one man, Don Bannister. Discovering, in an exhaustive library search, Kelly's abstruse two-volume tome, Bannister saw in it a revolutionary approach to the problem he was wrestling with – schizophrenic thought disorder. No topic could possibly have entailed a tougher test. In the consensus of the day, schizophrenia had been totally excluded from the possibility of psychological understanding, and relegated to the realm of psychopathology. The condition was viewed as intrinsically inexplicable, as simply the product of a destructive illness.

* Superior figures refer to the Notes, beginning on p. 129.

11

When Bannister succeeded in showing that thought disorder made sense – that the symptoms of schizophrenics could be understood in terms of their own understandings, their inner worlds – he dramatically demonstrated how fruitful Kelly's ideas could be.[3]

Don Bannister, who found in personal construct psychology such a rich vein of inspiration, himself inspired in many others a sense of its potential. Among these, I had the great good fortune to work closely with him during the 1960s in his research on schizophrenic thought disorder. Because his pioneering work was in the clinical field, it is in this sphere that, until quite recently, personal construct psychology has been developed. But over the last few years interest in the approach has been growing among people concerned with education. In one major line of research, Laurie Thomas has shown the fertility of Kelly's approach to the study of learning.[4] However, Thomas's work is addressed to a specialist audience. This is also the case with other psychologists, such as Maureen Pope,[5] who seek to demonstrate the relevance of this approach to teacher training and practice. For people directly engaged in schooling, there are as yet few sources.

One major reason why Kelly's approach seems likely to appeal to teachers is that, in personal construct psychology, the importance of learning has pride of place. Like most people who choose to teach, Kelly defines human possibility in essentially developmental terms. In his view, it is only by extending the meaning of our world that we may come to transform it. But this is not a facilely optimistic approach. Kelly himself was not just an academic psychologist, but a life-long practitioner of psychotherapy. And as a psychotherapist, he was well aware of how difficult it is to change. As against those humanistic writers who portray learning as painless, limitless personal growth, in this kind of psychology the learning process is often hard and sometimes costly. To those who struggle in schools with reluctant or alienated young people, a Kellyan picture may portray their own experience more recognizably than other humanistic writers.

Kelly's approach also accords closely with a growing movement in the teaching profession. Increasingly, teachers are coming to view themselves as experts in their own world. For too long the subjects of other people's researches, the evidence for questions not their own, those who teach are, more and more widely, acting to set up their own investigations, to define and pursue their own vital issues. For Kelly, in whose well-worn phrase each of us is our own personal scientist, such a movement could hardly be more appropriate, nor more timely.

That is why this book has been written as it has, in non-technical language (although for readers wishing to follow up specific aspects of personal construct psychology, notes are provided at the end of the book). Teachers, it is often said, are people much concerned with practicalities. Of all approaches, personal construct theory, grounded as it is in ordinary human experience, seems to represent that rare thing – 'nothing so practical as a good theory'. The book seeks to address the actual situation of those who work within the institutions of schooling. It acknowledges teachers as possessing their own expertise. Rather than proposing solutions, it suggests possible ways of looking at situations which may lead to their reconstruction. As never before, perhaps, teachers are now facing acute difficulties, agonizing dilemmas. For these, Kellyan psychology cannot hope to produce a panacea. Yet it may offer those who teach new and potentially helpful ways of engaging with problems in education.

This book is, therefore, an invitation to trainee and practising teachers, and those who work with them, to reconsider, from a fresh viewpoint, some critical issues in schooling. Where learning has been psychologically defined, this has typically been in terms that divorce it from the personal stance, the social engagements, of learners. In personal construct psychology, learning is itself a kind of stance, an engagement, however provisional, on the part of the learner. This carries major implications for the understanding, not just of classroom relationships, but of the process and content of learning itself. If it has spoken at length about learning, educational psychology has had little to say about teaching. But teaching, surely, is its own kind of social engagement, quite as diverse, quite as complex, as that of learning. And ultimately, the problems that teachers face may be more creatively tackled from a viewpoint which recognizes that, though transformation is never easy, human situations are open to change.

It may be helpful at this stage to set out a brief outline of the make-up of this book. The eight chapters follow a logic in which Kellyan ideas provide the framework for an examination of critical, and interrelated, aspects of the schooling enterprise. In being centred within the viewpoint of *teachers*, the book parts company with most educational texts, which locate their discussion in the position of *pupils*, relegating teachers and their situation to the sidelines. This does not, of course, imply a disregard of learners. Learning makes up the other half of the teaching equation. All teachers necessarily concern themselves with the individual identities, the developmental levels, the needs and struggles of the children they teach. If personal construct psychology has a contribution to make to teachers, it is in offering a particular kind of illumination of what *both* learning and teaching mean.

Because most trainee and practising teachers are unfamiliar with Kellyan ideas, the book begins with an introduction to personal construct psychology as it applies to the concerns of school. This approach defines both the learning and the teaching process as essentially constructive. Real learning, so far from being the reception of ready-made facts, entails the building of new personal meanings. As such, it can be, potentially, both a more exciting and a more dangerous activity than we generally assume. But teaching also, in its own way, involves the construction of meaning; and the teaching–learning encounter is, essentially, a meeting between the personal constructions, the subjective realities of teacher and pupil. This means that we cannot understand school learning without acknowledging *both* sorts of reality.

The next chapter, Teachers and teaching, takes this argument further. Traditionally, the activity of teaching has been seen in one of two ways. Either it has been defined in terms of skill; or else it has been viewed as the expression of particular personal qualities. Seldom has the *curriculum* been set at issue; though for teachers themselves, what they actually teach is usually of crucial importance. This chapter discusses not merely the 'how', and the 'who' of teaching, but also 'what' is taught. The curriculum of teaching, in the distinctive viewpoint of Kelly, is no ready-made, standard package of knowledge, but a personally constructed set of meanings which ramify, in subtle and complex ways, within the lives and identities of the teachers concerned.

In Chapter 3, Children's school stances, the focus is on the position of children as school pupils. From a Kellyan perspective, every social role represents a particular kind of engagement, a personal stance taken up towards the situation. In engaging themselves in the world of school, young children adopt widely different stances, as is clear from even the earliest days. The concern of this chapter is with how such divergent positions come to be adopted and the ways in which certain stances may all too easily become defined, on both sides, as deviant or antagonistic.

The next chapter, entitled Personal education, redefines this much-used term. For all that lip-service is generally paid to making learning personal, many schooling practices operate from the assumption that the highest kinds of knowledge, and educational modes, are impersonal. The personal, in practice, is often stigmatized. As teachers striving for integration of 'special' pupils are apt to find, personal needs in the classroom are generally identified with deviance and pathology. In the approach offered here, all learning, all learners, have to be seen in personal terms.

How learning actually occurs is the focus of Chapter 5, The process of learning. At issue here is the wayward, even paradoxical course of developing understanding. For Kelly, as for Piaget, even 'wrong' ideas make sense to those who hold them. And since confirmation and disconfirmation are crucial in how learning proceeds, teachers need to operate a delicate, personally sensitive balance between acknowledging the viability, pro-term, of existing formulations, and encouraging the learner to go further.

Many thoughtful writers about schooling have called attention to its hidden curriculum. This is the subject of the next chapter, The substrate of schooling. Looked at in Kellyan terms, the implicit political messages of school represent a basic substrate underlying what happens within the classroom world. If the hidden curriculum is ever to be transformed, this basic substrate will need to be made visible. Essentially, this means articulating the unacknowledged *psychology* that underlies both the official curriculum and classroom relations. Such concerns go well beyond personal–social education, and implicate every curriculum area.

The following chapter, Classroom relationships, examines something of this psychology in the sphere of pupil–teacher and pupil–pupil relations. These two spheres, it is suggested, are closely interlinked. In Kellyan terms, personal relationships flourish or founder to the extent that those involved can grasp each others' personal worlds. Where things go badly wrong between teachers and pupils, this may often arise out of gross failures in mutual comprehension. Conversely, teachers who foster the most positive classroom dynamics may be those who are most vividly conscious of the personal importance, for pupils themselves, of their own peer group relationships.

The final chapter is called The teaching situation. Here, the main ideas in the book are drawn together in an examination of the position of teachers in schooling. From a Kellyan viewpoint, the teaching situation is above all complex. Every classroom group contains multiple and heterogeneous subjectivities, each clamouring for personal acknowledgment. To this diverse world, teachers must bring a curriculum which is subject to demands, constraints and purposes not their own. Teaching, perhaps above any other professional activity, is the focus of constant pressures, contradictory demands from groupings both within and outside education. Hemmed in and beleaguered as they increasingly are, many teachers find scant opportunity for genuine professional development. Yet, as Kelly insisted, whatever exists can always be reconstrued. Even at such critically difficult times for education, there exist possibilities whereby teachers may work to reconstruct their situation. A Kellyan viewpoint, though it does not offer easy solutions, suggests that ultimately, there are grounds for hope.

1   A Kellyan approach

At the age of 14, alone among my classmates, I took up the option to study Latin. Over two years, for three periods a week, I had individual lessons with an elderly woman teacher. In the eccentric independent school I attended, this teacher was one of the few members of staff who had stayed for more than a couple of terms. Her main subject was Scripture, as it was then called. By the time I made my choice to study Latin with her, I knew this teacher very well. To the whole group of my contemporaries, she was a figure of fun, laughed at for her old-fashioned clothes and pedantic manner, cruelly compared with the vital and glamorous young women teachers who passed briefly through the school. Scripture, her subject, was held in very low esteem. The lessons were occasions in which we vied with each other in diverting this teacher from the material she had prepared. Since she treated every inquiry with earnest seriousness, and apparently never recognized flippant or mocking intentions, it was, in fact, very easy to alter the direction of her lessons.

My reasons for choosing to study Latin with this teacher had to do with her description of what the subject would entail. Inviting us to take up Latin, she spoke of Aeneas's mysterious journey, of the love poems of Catullus, of the dangerous political world which Cicero wrote about. It sounded like another version of English, which for me had been by far the most engrossing part of my school curriculum. And Latin, as taught by this teacher, did prove very much as I had anticipated. The texts we worked through were every bit as interesting, as moving, as human, as she had described them. My own progress in the subject also went well. Apparently impossible grammar seemed eventually, under this teacher's tuition, to become understandable. I found myself acquiring a large vocabulary, and even, sometimes, a sense of the rhythms of the language.

Yet, for all their interest and enjoyment, these Latin lessons involved complicated feelings. I found my own position ambiguous. Among my friends, I had for a long time played my part in maintaining and elaborating an unkind mockery of this particular teacher. Now, in my Latin lessons, I experienced unmistakable affection from her. I was caught up in her own wide learning and real love for the subject she was teaching. I found gradually that I could not enter into the public currency of jokes against her; Scripture lessons became increasingly painful occasions for me. My private learning, which made me 'special', was both treasured and embarrassing. It involved an experience of the teacher which could not be shared with friends who knew her very differently. The relationship set me apart, cut me off from my social group in this area of our school lives.

What was this learning about? To say that I learned Latin does not seem adequately to encompass it. I did develop an understanding of certain classical Latin texts. But this understanding was framed by the outlook of one particular teacher, coloured by her feelings, her unique sense of the meaning, the vitality of the writings. In coming to appreciate Virgil's poetry, I came to approach it from a particular angle, to take the direction towards it which my teacher somehow conveyed. By doing so, I necessarily changed my position towards the teacher herself, and this act subtly but irrevocably altered my position towards my friends. My learning – for all its interest and enjoyment, its opening of new horizons – was personally costly. It entailed complicated and painful feelings to do with loyalty and betrayal, solidarity and loneliness.

How, most basically, do we see education? A certain story, containing the essence of many age-old myths and fairy tales, is widely if implicitly shared. After an arduous search, a mysterious and sometimes dangerous journey, the brave and tenacious adventurer at last achieves his reward. He gains the keys of the kingdom. The world, with all its treasures – of knowledge, understanding, the whole cultural heritage – lies open to his taking. This is a story which sets the hardships, the confusion, the struggle of the learning endeavour against the richness of its prize. In its happy-ever-after ending, the learner who has stayed the whole long course, passed through each successive educational trial, triumphantly attains the ultimate goal – access to a world of understanding. It is in these terms that most of us usually see things. But what if we took another metaphor? Suppose we looked at the process of education as one version of the story of Adam and Eve.

For George Kelly, whose ideas have inspired this book, the biblical parable of Adam and Eve is the fundamental story of our humanity. In an essay entitled 'Sin and psychotherapy' (1979b),* he explores something of its meaning. The essay is a reflection on the situation of a middle-aged client who has sought all of his life to return to the Eden he knew in early childhood. But, like Adam, like all of us. he cannot go back. By eating the forbidden fruit, Adam and Eve have come to a knowledge of good and evil. And this is fateful knowledge. Through seeing moral possibilities where none existed before, we lose our simple delight in the way things are. The world cannot be accepted without question ever again; our knowledge of what might be makes us restless, keeps us searching. We can no longer take everything for granted. We now possess, for better or worse, 'the awful responsibility for distinguishing good from evil'. There is no going back to the innocence we shared with animals and birds, to the paradise of our pre-moral world.

In the story we usually tell of education, the quest ends when learners take their hard-earned reward, and, following arduous endeavours, come at last into their own. But if our story is of paradise lost, this is only the beginning. Knowledge has consequences. The story of Adam and Eve does not end with their eating of the apple – nor even with the expulsion from paradise which followed this. Knowing what they now know, Adam and Eve cannot but live out the moral possibilities they grasp:

With knowledge come responsibilities, and with responsibilities come trouble. Adam and Eve, in this remarkably insightful story, sought the knowledge of good and evil, and that is precisely what they got, for they lived to see one of their sons grow to be a good man, and the other his murderer (Kelly 1979b, quoted in Maher, pp. 166–7).

In such a view, knowledge is not the end of the story, but rather the beginning of a new, qualitatively different chapter. It is a chapter entailing the transformation of the character of

---

* Full references quoted in the text are contained in the References beginning on p. 133.

the protagonist. The questing knight of the traditional tale does not himself change when at last his mission is accomplished. But Adam and Eve are irrevocably altered by the knowledge they acquire. Adam begins to experience a new disturbing self-consciousness. Once happily unaware of himself as a separate being, he now finds he is alone and embarrassingly exposed; he sees with shame that he must cover his nakedness. In coming to know the world differently, we ourselves are transformed.

We think of knowledge, insight, understanding, as worthwhile in altogether simple ways. For learners struggling with their task, the treasures to be gained are of pure gold. Skies are cloudless in the kingdom of understanding. Yet, like Adam, we may find that we must buy our knowledge dearly. What we know may make us lonely in our social worlds; it may impose responsibilities we would far rather not have. It is not only martyrs, who, like Galileo, may have to suffer for what they come to know. The small girl whose elder brother insists on proving to her that Father Christmas is an illusion, must give up a specially delightful part of her early childhood. Christmas is forever changed; the magic cannot be recaptured. To those British people for whom the Second World War was the noble struggle of a brave little island under its heroic leader, later revelations of the bombing of Dresden, the betrayal of the Cossacks, were wholly repugnant, representing knowledge to be acquired only with the greatest reluctance.

In Kelly's model, our personal construct systems define the understanding we each live by. This means that learning is never the acquisition of a single, isolated bit of knowledge. Our ways of seeing things are inextricably intertwined. To alter one assumption means that others, too, are brought into question. Understanding has implications; a change in one idea entails possibilities of having to rethink others. And this is just as true of school knowledge as of informal understanding. If art is really just a matter of colour, where does this leave all those careful pencil drawings you do at home, to the pleasure and admiration of your parents? Does this exciting new approach to maths render invalid all your earlier understanding of computational problems? Or, now that you begin to see how human affairs have always been affected by race, gender, social class, must the whole of history be rethought?

Some of the implications of learning involve risks that extend into the future. If, as a girl, you pursue your present fascination with molecular theory, where will it take you? Doing a physics option will put you among boys, and lead you in directions very different from those your friends are taking. If you follow up these interesting English studies, with consequences for the way you speak, you may find that you have become alienated from your own background. Going on with your guitar lessons might entail the possibility of discovering, in the end, that you cannot make it to the top.

As Adam found, to live by understanding rather than obedience means entering the difficult realm of existential choice. We have to give up the security of ignorance – the known boundaries to thinking and experience, the safety of shared ideas, the comfort of taking things for granted. Nor is it only individual 'learners' whose security is threatened by new ways of knowing. Societies are grounded in shared assumptions about human reality. To call any of those basic assumptions into question is to risk moving beyond the pale – into martyrdom, or madness. For most of us, such possibilities are very remote. But even much more limited extensions of understanding inevitably entail a questioning of conventional ideas, a refusal to be bound by traditional, established assumptions. As such, they pose their own challenge to the status quo.

In Kelly's philosophy, we construct and reconstruct what we know about ourselves and our world. Yet this does not, I think, presuppose that each of us must recreate the wheel. Knowledge does not exist only in our heads; it is also out there, enshrined in laws, in cultural artefacts, in established practices. Though understanding arises only out of the interrogations that human beings put to their world, once acquired, it takes on a kind of independent existence, an authority. Cumulatively, it provides the whole frame of reference within which we, as individuals, construct the meaning of our experience. No one can step outside his or her culture, or develop terms that simply bypass its frame of reference. Yet cultural understandings differ across space and time. What we know, we know as members of a culture which has its own distinctive interpretations of reality. But these interpretations can never be final, only provisional. They remain open, potentially, to change. In every epoch, through the struggle of individuals and groups, new themes, new issues become salient, with consequent changes in social practice.

As Kelly insists, construct systems are personal. But this

does not make them solipsistic. Though each of us inhabits a unique experiential world, psychological meanings must, if they are to be viable, be built together with others. The human enterprise depends on a shared social reality. The sense we make of our lives must also make some sense to others. And since human realities are, first and foremost, *social* realities, personal meanings have their essential currency in relations between people, rather than within some private, individual world. From the very beginning of life, interpretations – the meanings to be accorded to things – are offered and exchanged between infants and their caregivers. As babies grow into childhood, the conversational confirmations, challenges, comparisons, interrogations of personal meaning develop at a geometrical rate. A widening social experience brings awareness of competing realities, alternative constructions. Somehow these must be met and negotiated. A personal system of meaning has to be forged which is viable, liveable, yet which remains open rather than closed.

Education, in this psychology, is the systematic interface between personal construct systems. This view of formal learning puts as much emphasis on teachers' personal meanings as on those of learners. Here, a Kellyan approach stands apart from most educational psychology, which, while generally focusing on the distinctive ways in which individual *pupils* see things, tends to lump *teachers* together. The knowledge they represent, the meanings they offer are, it is implied, essentially standard. Underlying this definition of teachers, in terms of a standardized curriculum, are certain absolutist assumptions about knowledge itself. If we believe that history, science or maths embody particular ultimate truths about the world, then we can see all teachers of these subjects as representing essentially the same sort of expertise. But we cannot take this view if knowledge is provisional. Learning, from this perspective, is not a matter of acquiring what Kelly dubs 'nuggets of truth', a treasure-house of human certainties. In learning, we cannot ever achieve final answers; rather we find new questions, we discover other possibilities which we might try out. Knowledge is ultimately governed by constructive alternativism; everything can always be reconstrued. Reality is not to be pinned down forever in a standardized school curriculum. The understanding that teachers offer is essentially provisional – for the time being. And, for all that school knowledge has high social consensus and is grounded in the whole cultural heritage, it is necessarily *personal*. It has its significance within the personal construct system of the particular teacher. Since each person inhabits a distinctive world of meaning, the curriculum of education is constructed afresh, and individually, by every teacher who offers it.

Our personal construct systems carry what, in the broadest possible sense, each of us knows. It is these systems which allow us to 'read' our lives psychologically. They locate us, moment to moment, within events. They define the stances we take. They represent our possibilities of action, the choices we can make. They embody the dimensions of meaning which give form to our experience, the kind of interpretation which we cast upon events. Since none of us can know anything of the world, except through the meanings we have available to us, the dimensions we have constructed – our constructs – are crucially important. Of course these dimensions of meaning are not isolated and separate. Our experience of the world is complex, all-of-a-piece, rather than a succession of different and unrelated categorizations. Constructs are essentially interwoven within a personal system of meaning.

It is this interrelationship that produces the richness of implication, the complexity, the depth of any human perception. Seeing her new class, the experienced teacher instantly gets the feeling of a tricky group. The perception carries with it a whole network of other interpretations – of past experience, future expectations, possible strategies, potential outcomes. These constructions define the teacher's position towards the class group, her assumptions about them, the kinds of engagement possible for her. They are likely to be available to her not as explicit, verbal labels, but rather as an implicit set of guidelines towards the situation, felt and sensed rather than put inwardly into words. Our construct systems encompass much more of what we know than we could ever say; and the more fundamental the knowledge, the less easily accessible it probably is to explicit verbalization.

All this gives an overriding importance to the network of personal meaning which those who teach and learn bring to educational contexts. Nor is this just a matter of academic definition. As a man who combined with his university appointments a life-long involvement in psychotherapy, Kelly himself needed to develop practical strategies for eliciting personal meaning. The latent, intuitive, experiential issues involved in personal distress and breakdown have to be acknowledged, made explicit, before they can be explored and reflected upon. And it was to elicit this very personal, intimate material, that Kellyan techniques were developed.[1] Such techniques are, above all else, *conversational*. This means not only that they are essentially informal, but that they are rooted in a credulous rather than a judging attitude to what is offered. They are committed to listening, if possible, to what is *not*, as well as what *is* said, to hearing something of the connotations surrounding particular constructions.

For most people familiar with personal construct psychology, it is the repertory grid technique[2] which defines this approach *par excellence*. This is essentially a categorization, or sorting task, in which a number of items are judged in terms of dimensions that can be applied to them. From statistical associations among the judgements made, conceptual linkages are inferred. I have found that a much simpler approach is often equally fruitful, and avoids many of the problems associated with repertory grids. Truer to genuine conversation, it does not force the person into making judgements which feel artificial, which do violence to natural ways of thinking. Nor does it remove the material offered, to be submitted privately for statistical analysis. The interpretation of what the material may mean remains open, as much the property of the subject as are the initial constructions. For want of a better title, I call this technique the Salmon Line.

When children are introduced to new areas of the school curriculum, they make their own sense of what is presented to them. A few years ago, I was involved in studying a second-year design and technology class (Salmon and Claire 1984).[3] In order to compare the perceptions of the children with those of their teacher, I asked both to talk about this school subject in relation to a line:

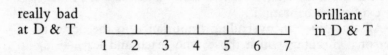

really bad   brilliant
at D & T   1   2   3   4   5   6   7   in D & T

First, I invited all the pupils to make a mark on the line which they felt represented where they stood at the moment in general competence in the subject. Had they always been at this point, or somewhere lower? Again, I asked for a mark to show where. What point on the line did they expect to reach eventually? Having obtained these judgements, I then asked the children to flesh them out for me. What could they do now in D & T that they had not been able to do when they stood lower? How had they come to be able to do these things, not having been able to do them before? What would they be able to do in future that they could not do now, and again, how would this happen? Then I invited the children to place on the line someone they knew who was very competent, and someone who was very incompetent, in D & T. Again, I asked them to illustrate these judgements, and to explain how it was that these individuals were so competent, or so incompetent. The teacher's task was essentially similar, except that I asked him to make judgements only about the pupils, rather than including himself.

Out of all this material emerged some profound differences in the ways in which this particular teacher and his classroom group perceived the meaning of their D & T lessons. For the teacher, the D & T curriculum entailed, above all, the development of designing capacity. He saw this as a process of imaginative construction and reconstruction – a process essentially involving collaboration, in which pupils could try out and compare ideas, exchange and challenge possible designs. For him, the curriculum had room for personal creativeness, and was open to every pupil. All this gave only secondary significance to technical skills, and to the particular artefact produced.

To the children, their D & T lessons meant something very different. Almost universally, they defined progression in the curriculum in terms of the kind of artefact produced. They saw their learning as developing from 'make-believe', 'practice' objects like model bridges, to objects that were usable and 'for real', such as shelves. This valuation stood in direct opposition to the teacher's priorities, which set the imaginative power needed to construct a model bridge a long way above the purely mechanical skills involved in making a shelf. For the children, the D & T workshop was a kind of assembly plant in miniature. They did not see their work as creative, but judged technical skills to be of paramount importance. Concomitantly, the learning process was seen as one of individual effort and practice, rather than involving collaboration.

But most children, far from seeing progress as open, viewed competence as largely inborn, with female gender representing an insuperable barrier.

This kind of material is easily elicited by the simple device of using a line to talk about the process and the curriculum of learning. And, as material, it seems very important. We all 'read' situations according to the meaning we give them, the interpretations we make about them. To the children in this particular group, learning, in their D & T workshop, meant something rather different from the meaning with which their teacher invested it. They read their own significance into what they were asked to do; they judged the success, the progress of their work in their own, different terms. To this extent, despite the generally positive atmosphere of this classroom, teacher and pupils were to a large extent bypassing each other.

The elicitation of personal meaning, by techniques such as these, can potentially forestall mutual misreading in learning situations. And this is not just a matter of the more cognitive aspects of construing. In Kellyan philosophy, feelings do not represent a separate, special category of experience, but consist of the encounters between our networks of personal meaning, and particularly significant events. This is not, of course, the way we usually look at things. Traditionally, we see feelings as lying outside the domain defined as learning. Either they belong to the 'personality' of the learner, or they arise out of the social context, the interrelationships which provide the setting for learning. We have generally two different currencies for talking about the emotional and intellectual aspects of experience. All this appears otherwise if we take the view that, in learning, we come to alter our own personal stance towards our worlds.

The personal adjustments which are entailed in any learning that is not merely superficial often have deep and complicated ramifications. The new position towards things must be followed through. Familiar, comfortable, safe attitudes may have to be discarded. We may find ourselves out on a limb, possessing knowledge which those around cannot share, may find suspect or incomprehensible. Changes in understanding bring us into new relations with others. Perhaps, in the end, we ourselves cannot sustain our new 'knowledge', because it cannot be reconciled with the fundamental assumptions we need to live by. Given the complexity of developing personal understanding, it hardly seems surprising that, in most learning situations, problems arise involving what are undeniably feelings. In a Kellyan approach, feelings are necessarily integral with learning.

The affective component in learning does, of course, embrace positive as well as negative feelings. It is Carl Rogers (1983), above all, who has documented the joy, the excitement, the sense of personal freedom, which can arise when people extend the horizons of their understanding. For Rogers, learning means affirming deep organismic inner promptings. To follow freely where these promptings lead, rather than merely conforming in order to please others, allows human beings to discover their own innate potential for personal growth. For most people who reflect on their own learning, such feelings are personally recognizable. In reconstruing some aspect of ourselves and our lives, things suddenly fall into place. Huge possibilities of understanding present themselves. It seems that where, before, we could see dimly or not at all, there is suddenly meaning – meaning which connects things up in exciting ways.

But learning is not always like this. New understanding is, potentially, threatening. Subjectively, the experience of threat tends to take one of two forms: anxiety or hostility. To be confronted with an unfamiliar curriculum can result in a feeling of complete bewilderment. You feel totally at sea, lost, without anchors of any kind, unable to relate what is being offered to personally meaningful interpretations. This is the experience of being unable to engage with learning because it is impossible even to formulate a question. In Kelly's terms, anxiety means a lack of implication. Where what is presented seems to bear no relation to any of one's own ways of making sense of things, there is no possibility of grasping it, no sense of its connotations.

It seems likely that no one who has gone through formal education has escaped this sense of acute discomfort, disorientation and personal alienation. But there is surely another, equally familiar way of experiencing the threat implicit in learning. Where the position entailed in novel understanding seems to run directly counter to one's basic, known, habitual position, the reaction may well be one of hostility. As Tom Ravenette has remarked,[4] teachers often prove what pupils cannot afford to have proved – and vice versa. The invitation to recast a question in 'proper English' may, unwittingly, ride roughshod over the personal identity and pride of the black adolescent. Far too much is at stake for this young learner to accept the reconstruction of his classroom language. Instead, he must seize the situation, turn it around, prove to his mates and himself the hollowness of the teacher's authority. Or, perhaps, the teacher 'reads' this student's bearing and manner as provocative and disrespectful. His own vital sense of himself as a teacher seems to be under threat. He can only take drastic action to reverse this apparent implication: by exercising his ultimate sanction as a teacher, he may be able to exclude the threat altogether.

In a Kellyan view, hostility[5] represents a desperate effort to maintain a personally vital position by cooking the books, refusing to accept evidence which seems to invalidate that position. Whereas, in anxiety,[6] we remain outside the area of reconstruction, hovering nearby, aware only of our own incomprehension, in hostility we engage in an active manoeuvre towards it, seizing the situation and trying to force it into something we can accept. This definition takes the perspective of the subject, and focuses on what things mean for the anxious or the hostile person, rather than on the uncomfortable effects they may have on others. Because this approach avoids what Kelly calls 'the language of complaint', it seems to offer more possibilities for learners and teachers to understand, to expect, and perhaps to work through the diffi- cult feelings entailed in real personal learning.

Making sense of negative feelings was, in fact, necessary for Kelly as a psychotherapist committed to helping his clients reconstrue their lives. And – as he announced in his often- quoted comparison of psychotherapy clients and research students[7] – he insisted that both sorts of people are engaged in essentially the same quest. That quest he defined as serious inquiry. Those who work as clients must struggle to make sense out of their personal suffering, their guilt, their existential confusion. This necessarily entails the effort to reflect carefully, honestly, on the implications of personal experience. What does such experience mean for one's own real position in life? It may be necessary to dare new ways of looking at life, to see things in altered terms, engage with events on a different basis. But where does this leave former values, previous experience? If we are to keep faith with our past selves, then earlier assumptions cannot simply be discarded or denied. We have instead to revise our previous position, to see our basic values in new terms, give them a different kind of meaning.

All this does, of course, represent the deepest kind of learning. And those engaged in formal education can also sometimes come to an understanding which is profound, rich in implication, and personally meaningful. Yet in neither situation are these outcomes commonplace. Many people who come for psychotherapeutic help remain imprisoned, unable to escape, in Kelly's terms, the shackles of their circumstances, or choosing, in the end, the security of known misery over the frightening openness of freedom. Even those who bring to their inquiries a conscious and urgent need to take their understanding further, do not always find it possible to reconstruct the basis of their living. For children and young people in formal education, the basis of their inquiry as learners is very different; they lack the initiative of psychotherapeutic clients. School learners do not choose to come to school, let alone decide their own curriculum.

Although in psychotherapy and in official learning the essential quest may be the same, teachers do, perhaps, face a harder task in many ways. Engaging reluctant young people in official learning is very different from responding to the intense demands of troubled, searching people. Given that the school curriculum is far from open, that much of the prescribed content of learning seems to many pupils a long way from their daily life experience, it is no easy matter for teachers to link up personally vital issues with classroom materials and activities. Whereas the responsibilities of psychotherapists are to their clients, and more broadly to their profession, teachers are accountable to many and divergent groupings, and subject to increasingly insistent and conflicting pressures. Our schooling system serves a society which is itself deeply divided: the demands on teachers are, perhaps, ultimately irreconcilable.

A Kellyan account of learning does not offer a panacea, a simple solution to intractable problems. Yet in its refusal to oversimplify the nature of the learning process, its insistence on the personal character of coming to know, its perspective on 'problems' as integral to learning, this approach does, perhaps, both endorse and elaborate the first-hand, intuitive understanding of those who teach.

2 Teachers and teaching

Ask anyone about their most significant experiences in learning, and they will almost certainly start talking about the people who taught them. That awkward, memorable young man, whose own ardent passion for mathematics created from a dry-as-dust subject a distinctive, fascinating world. The woman English teacher, with her undaunted faith in you, which finally allowed you to break through your writing block. The brilliant and sarcastic person who exposed your early attempts at painting to public ridicule, and left you permanently and hopelessly convinced of your own artistic ineptitude. For very many people, teachers seem to have been the key that opened – or locked – the door to personally meaningful kinds of learning. Nor is this only a retrospective feeling. In children's talk of daily classroom experience, the figures of their teachers loom large. And for children at school, teachers are not at all much-of-a-muchness, but are highly differentiated. This is the case for primary as well as secondary age, for boys as for girls, and for pupils alienated from school work as for highly motivated pupils. All children, in their experiences of classroom learning, seem to have a keen sense of their teachers as very different, distinctive kinds of people. This sense of difference is typically quite complex, and goes a long way beyond merely feeling that some teachers are good and others are bad. In discussing any teacher, children convey something of a particular personal world, a world with its own kind of atmosphere, its own possibilities. It is a world where certain things can happen, where certain expectations operate. It is also a world in which you experience particular kinds of feeling, and even become a particular kind of person.

When teachers are the focus in educational writing and research, the central question is, typically, what are the differences between effective and ineffective teachers. What is it that enables some people to teach well, to motivate their pupils, to facilitate understanding, a grasp of the curriculum, while others succeed only in producing confusion, boredom, antagonism? In addressing this question, educationists have, of course, adopted a variety of approaches. It does not seem too simplistic, however, to group these into two broadly different views. One of these sees teacher effectiveness in terms of skill; the other, in terms of personality.

The first of these two views, which defines effectiveness as skill, has probably been in many ways the more directly influential. It is supported by a large body of research in schools. Much of this work has been summarized by Morrison and McIntyre (1972). Traditionally this research has been based on an explicit and careful delineation of the criteria of teaching effectiveness. If teachers are competent, so the argument goes, then certain measurable outcomes can be expected from their teaching. The level of reading skill achieved, the number of information items retained, the comprehension level demonstrated: such indices of pupil learning can be taken to constitute the measure of teacher competence. Significant features of teaching behaviour can, using the same argument, be defined and assessed in equally quantifiable ways. The way teachers structure their material, organize pupil tasks, or give feedback on performance: these aspects can be carefully monitored and recorded. Or the focus may be more fine-grained, with the researcher's attention given to quite specific features of teacher–pupil interaction. One much-used measuring instrument, the Flanders Analysis of Interaction Categories, represents a coding system for analysing kinds of teacher-talk: giving praise, accepting pupils' ideas, questioning, giving directions, and so on. In the rationale of this kind of work, it is the statistical relationships between particular measurable features of teacher behaviour, on the one hand, and particular measurable educational outcomes, on the other, that tell us what are the characteristics of good teachers.

A book by John Powell, *The Teacher's Craft* (1985), illustrates one current line of work within this perspective. In a large-scale study of teaching in Scottish primary schools, Powell set out to define the characteristics which both differentiated between classrooms and affected pupil performance. A special, quite complex observation schedule was compiled. Using this schedule, observers made copious notes from five observations each day of teachers' classroom practice. Particular teaching categories were then coded from judgements summating these observations. One category, for instance, defined whether teacher control was direct or indirect. Another related to whether or not teachers fostered a sense of responsibility in their pupils. Where pupil performance was concerned, assessments were made of attitudes, on the one hand, and mathematical achievements, on the other. However, although the study succeeded in demonstrating measurable differences in teaching skills, the statistical correlations between these differences and variations in pupil attitudes or achievements showed no very clear-cut relationships.

What kind of answers have come from research studies into teaching skill? Broadly speaking, they have highlighted the importance of certain organizational aspects, on the one hand, and of particular interactional features, on the other. As they emerge from this kind of research, effective teachers seem to be those who organize their material, structure it into manageable chunks, pace their work to pupil progress, make task demands explicit, and give clear feedback. They are managerially skilled. In interaction, they accept, and make use of pupil initiatives, beyond merely instructing them; they interact with all pupils rather than with just a small sub-group of them.

It is to this last sphere of behaviour that most recent research within this perspective has increasingly turned. As awareness has grown of the diversity within the average classroom – of the presence of disaffected as well as motivated pupils, of learning difficulties alongside learning breakthroughs – so researchers have been more and more concerned with the question of teachers' differential engagements with particular pupil sub-groups. So rather than producing generalized measures of the nature of teacher–pupil interaction, the research has taken note, for instance, of the uneven proportion of teacher time given to boys as against girls, or to boisterous as against quieter pupils. Such studies, in becoming increasingly attentive to the whole classroom, have tended to move away from precisely measurable indices of teachers' interactions with their pupils, and instead to adopt more global and impressionistic assessments. By the same token, educational outcomes have become defined in less concrete, literal ways.

This body of work, which defines teaching as skill, has made its educational impact in a number of ways. Not only has it provided a perspective on teaching – a way of thinking about the differences between competent and incompetent teachers.

It has also offered a good deal that is practical, that can be used in initial or in-service training. For the many people who see training as the acquisition of relevant skills, this approach is immediately useful. Its findings have pointed to the importance of organizational aspects of teaching, of crucial differences in the detail of teachers' communications with pupils, of teachers' need to maintain active monitoring of the classroom and so on. In their initial training, student teachers can be helped to develop skills such as these, for instance through the experiential learning of micro-teaching. For, as many people have found, seeing your own behaviour on videotape can reveal some very surprising things, showing you aspects of yourself of which you were quite unaware. Through this medium, some student teachers have realized, to their own dismay, how much they talk, how little they listen; while others discover, with equal consternation, that it is always to male learners, never to female ones, that they address their questions.

Yet for all its apparent good sense, its useful practical implications, many educationalists have reservations about this approach. For such people, the idea that good teaching can be finally pinned down as a set of observable competences is ultimately not convincing. Some would say that fine teachers are born, not made by the acquisition of precisely definable skills. What gives their teaching its power is something essentially mysterious, which cannot be reduced to a laundry list.

A very different perspective is that of the Rogerian school. Here, teaching is viewed, not as a matter of instruction, but as the facilitation of the learner's innate striving to develop. Because to develop as a human being often seems difficult and risky, no one can really learn outside a context of personal trust, personal support. So the qualities which the teachers need are those of a caring and sensitive friend.

For Rogers, indeed, good teachers are good to the extent that they refuse to act like teachers:

To my surprise I found that my classrooms became more exciting places of learning as I ceased to be a *teacher*. It wasn't easy. It happened rather gradually, but as I began to trust students, I found they did incredible things in their communication with each other, in their learning of content material in the course, in blossoming out as growing human beings. Most of all they gave me courage to be myself more freely, and this led to profound interaction. They told me their feelings. They raised questions I had never thought about. I began to sparkle with emerging ideas that were new and exciting to me, but also, I found, to them (Rogers, 1983, p. 26).

Perhaps unsurprisingly, Carl Rogers himself has spent most of his professional life as a practising psychotherapist. Rogers, like Kelly, sees no fundamental difference between good teaching and good psychotherapy. Just as the therapy client is anxious that others may find him wanting, and dare not trust his own experience, so, Rogers believes, the person blocked in learning is afraid to feel what she really feels, to follow her own directions, for fear this might lose her the approval, the affection, of others. Both people can be liberated through exactly the same experience. Each shares their most secret, most incoherent, most seemingly shameful feelings with another person, and finds that that person recognizes them for what they are, yet passes no judgement on them and continues to value and cherish them. By living through this experience, clients and learners acquire a sense of real security, a solid belief in themselves, a trust in their own feelings. The blocks in living, in learning have melted away; the person has regained the innate human capacity for growth.

Given that learners are seen as needing this kind of experience, how does the Rogerian approach define good teachers? To establish a relationship which is both genuinely sensitive and genuinely supportive, very special personal qualities are needed. Rogers describes the ideal teacher as possessing the capacity for empathy with others, as able to 'read' another's feelings accurately. Such a person also needs great warmth of feeling, and the ability to sustain affection despite occasional moments of irritation. But finally, the teacher must be an honest, truthful person, not someone who puts on a false front from time to time. If teachers pretend to feel what they do not feel, or disguise their real responses, they cannot hope to inspire learners to trust their own deepest feelings.

All this, as most people would see it, has to do with personality, rather than training. The Rogerian school of thought certainly does emphasize the crucial importance of personality in the make-up of a good teacher. But this does not mean that training has no part to play. Even the warmest, most honest, most sensitive person could not simply embark on psychotherapeutic practice without some sort of prior training. In this philosophy, the right kind of training for teachers is, again, essentially that of therapists. Those who are personally well-qualified to establish truly facilitative relationships will come to develop these qualities still further through experiencing such a relationship for themselves. People undergoing a Rogerian kind of teacher training, like trainee therapists, go through a kind of apprenticeship as learners, within the relationship which they will eventually set up as teachers for other learners. The contexts of their development, like the contexts of Rogerian learning generally, may include encounter group experience as well as one-to-one counselling.

The impact of this view of teachers and teaching has, of course, been rather different from the impact of the skills approach. On a practical level, given the UK educational system, the specific teaching modes proposed by Rogers are not readily feasible, although his suggestions, particularly for experiential group learning, are often used in counselling and pastoral work. Nor do Rogerian principles directly inform the training of teachers. Warmth, honesty and empathy with others may be qualities valued by those who select candidates for training; but certainly most training courses are a long way away from the intimate, deeply personal exploration advocated by this school. Yet if Rogerian methods are not necessarily directly translatable, the Rogerian philosophy about teachers has certainly been a source of inspiration for many people. The emphasis on the crucial place of feeling in education, on the inescapably personal nature of learning – this has radically changed our conceptions of what teaching entails. If learning is a personal affair, then so must teaching be. The person of the teacher may be just as important a factor as that of the learner, and in the personal relation between the two may lie the key to the whole learning enterprise.

In their different ways, each of these schools of thought has illuminated our ideas about what teachers do, and about what teaching means. Yet both schools are strangely silent about one crucial aspect – the content of teaching. In the one approach, we see teachers as highly skilled organizers, monitoring and controlling pupils, adeptly changing gear to direct and manage classroom activities. Yet what is it all about, what is it actually for? In the other approach, the picture is of a deeply under-standing, caring friend, who listens, responds, encourages the learner towards the honesty and confidence needed to venture into real learning. But learning about what? In neither approach does the discussion of teaching entail discussion of the curriculum. The first model implies a generalized body of knowledge, independent of the particular competence, the critical skills, of the person offering it. The Rogerian model, on the other hand, assumes the content of learning to be entirely governed by the learner.

To teachers themselves, what they teach is surely not a matter of indifference. Trying to explain his wish to teach, the young student teacher refers to his enthusiasm for his subject, his sense that children, too, could find it interesting, exciting. As the primary teacher discusses tomorrow's plans for her class, it is the value, the significance, of the work she hopes the children will do, that she emphasizes most. And looking back over his teaching career, reflecting on its triumphs, its disappointments, the retiring head of English dwells on the English curriculum. How difficult it was to change from the old way, the single standard form of grammar and pronunciation, to be mastered by every child! Then, you knew what you were doing, what you were aiming at; you could tell children when they had got things right. And yet this new way, for all you resisted it at the time, proved in the end so much better, with its recognition of linguistic diversity, thereby acknowledging all children's language, giving every child a place in the classroom.

The same concern with content emerges from the first-person accounts of teachers who have written about their work. Herbert Kohl, for instance, in his book *36 Children* (1971), vividly describes his efforts to teach reading to a class of alienated youngsters. The motive force, the impetus that kept him struggling day after day with bored and hostile children, was his own conviction that being able to read is wonderfully liberating, that reading can open doors into new worlds, create possibilities for living that did not exist before. And in the end, Kohl's breakthrough came when he shared this belief with his reluctant class. He told his pupils *why* he wanted them to be able to read, what reading had meant to him, what it might do for them – and what not being able to read might do to them, and to their lives.

For an approach that takes subjectivity seriously, an understanding of teachers is not possible if it takes no account of the curriculum they teach. As distinct from the approaches we have considered so far, the Kellyan view, with its emphasis on the personal construction of meaning, is likely to have a good deal to say about the content which teachers themselves see as so important. So, far from describing a teacher in terms distinct from his or her curriculum, in the perspective of personal construct psychology you are yourself, in some sense, what you teach.

What would it mean to take this approach, to see the content of teaching as intrinsically personal to each particular teacher? Teaching would be viewed, not as the passing on of a parcel of objective knowledge, but as the attempt to share what you yourself find personally meaningful. It is the teacher's own sense of the richness of history, the wonder of the physical world, that makes the lesson exciting; where pupils catch fire, it is the teacher's fire they catch. And it is a uniquely personal fire. One teacher's Spanish is not the Spanish of her colleague; though the syllabus may be the same, the lessons are not. What gives importance, value, vitality to one person's material is hers alone; and it is this – or its absence – which is the real substance of her teaching.

For, as everyone knows, not all teaching is exciting, and lessons may be very boring, for teachers as well as for children. If we think about the personal nature of the curriculum, it does not really seem surprising that teachers are often personally uncomfortable with the content of their teaching. This is not just a matter of gradually losing a sense of the liveliness of the subject through years and years of daily classroom grind. Since the freedom of teachers is very much constrained, particularly through traditional examination boards, it is not at all uncommon to find teachers obliged to put over a curriculum which they do not like, do not respect, and do not personally value. For many people who teach in schools, the resources and texts which constitute much of the curriculum also impose unacceptable limits and assumptions on what may be taught. How is it possible, when you are all too aware of the exploitation of colonialism and its dire consequences for many children in your multicultural classroom, to teach history from books which glorify British explorers, British conquests? The educational status quo responds slowly and reluctantly to pressures for curriculum reform; in the meantime teachers must prepare their pupils for examinations on the traditional syllabus. There are also other kinds of alienation for those who teach. A young teacher of biology, keenly aware of animal rights, can only feel a constant inner protest if she works in an old-fashioned department which still routinely dissects animal corpses. For a home economics teacher strongly concerned to engage boys in her curriculum, the school system which forces a choice between her subject and design and technology must impose a meaning on her classroom work which runs counter to her own values.

If teaching means offering others your personal sense of the curriculum, then feelings of alienation from what you teach have to be taken seriously. What such feelings may mean is conveyed by a piece of research carried out recently by two psychologists working in London, Rosie Walden and Valerie Walkerdine (1985). Walden and Walkerdine were interested in exploring how it is that girls, who start off as good, or even better than boys in maths gradually fall behind and generally end up mathematically incompetent. There has, of course, been much concern with this question, which many people have seen as one part of the gender stereotyping of school knowledge. Maths and science are seen as objective, high-level, high-status, and essentially male subjects, while languages, art, child development, are seen as altogether softer and less rigorous kinds of subject – for girls rather than boys. Part of this stereotyping is the whole process whereby men typically end up teaching the 'male' subjects, and women, the 'female' ones. So one solution has been to reverse this logic, and to employ, for instance, women maths teachers.

It was this situation which Walden and Walkerdine examined. They studied the position of female maths teachers, talking to them about their work and watching them in their classrooms. What emerged showed how complicated it is for a woman to teach maths. This is partly because the curriculum of school maths has its own kind of gender-related content. In the early stages of primary maths, problems are located in the domestic world – the traditional sphere of girls and women. But gradually this changes, so that by secondary age the content is stereotypically male – the world of mechanics and engineering. What does this mean for a woman teaching maths?

In the early stages, in her classroom work with boys and girls, the primary maths teacher is, in a sense, 'at home' with the subject. The problems she discusses with her pupils are those of her own traditional domain. 'In early mathematics, domestic tasks (weighing, measuring, shopping) are used as a matter of course. This allows stereotypically feminine activities to be used as the site for the teaching of mathematics.' These activities are part of the whole world with which the teacher, as a woman, is likely to be very familiar. They relate to spheres which the boys and girls in her class expect her to know about, to be expert in. But later, in the secondary classroom, things are different. The female maths teacher is now talking about areas of experience with which she is likely to be rather unfamiliar, to feel something of a stranger. And even if this is not so, for the pupils in her class these areas do not belong to her. Nor do they, by now, belong to the girls there; they are part of the whole domain claimed by the boys.

Another aspect of the ambiguous position occupied by these women arises out of their place in the authority structure of the school. Just as the highest status is typically accorded to subjects defined as male, so those holding positions of relative power in the secondary school system tend to be men rather than women. This is true all the way from the post of head-teacher, to the level of ancillary staff, where a man will typically hold the post of caretaker, as against the humbler post of cleaner typically occupied by a woman. For a woman who teaches maths, the authority given to her by the high status of her subject is at the same time subtly undermined by her own gender.

From what Walden and Walkerdine saw, all this had a profound influence on the way these women taught. In contrast to their general confidence and ease in primary classrooms, many women maths teachers in the secondary school context were clearly uneasy, diffident, uncertain of their role. This sense of insecurity was most obvious in their dealings with boys, towards whom they tended to be deferential, even apologetic. Of course, something of this discomfort was communicated to the pupils, thereby reinforcing the very message which teaching appointments like these are meant to counter.

If the curriculum to be taught were really separate from the particular teacher who offers it, then setting up women to teach maths would solve, once and for all, the problem of its gender stereotyping. The fact that this solution turns out to be far from simple, and may sometimes actually make things worse, must mean that what people teach is inseparable from who they are. A personal construct psychology, with its view of everything as personal, cannot make the traditional separation between teachers and what they teach. This means that, in its terms, the curriculum of teaching is not an independent entity: teachers and their expertise are essentially interlinked.

We usually talk about expertise in a subject as though it were a question of the mastery of a standard body of material: the sequence of recorded historical events, or the interrelated principles of physics. We imagine that, apart from slight differences in emphasis, two experts possess essentially the same knowledge, have their identical insider's view. Yet such an assumption cannot fit with the idea that knowledge is essentially a construction. George Kelly is not, of course, the originator of this idea, which, for some time now has been put forward by sociologists of knowledge. In 1967, *The Social Construction of Reality* by Peter Berger and Thomas Luckmann, argued the case in a particularly persuasive way. In their account, growing up in our families entails becoming socialized into a particular construction of the world. This construction is, for each of us, what we take entirely for granted, as being simply reality. It is what we have assimilated from our parents and others without any explicit teaching on their part; in fact we should find it very difficult to put into words at all. The formal learning we engage in, our deliberate later attempts to extend our understanding – what Berger and Luckmann call secondary socialization – this relates to much less profound, potentially much more precarious levels of knowledge. Whereas primary socialization entails social constructions intimately shared and lived out among members of a close social unit, the social constructions of secondary socialization are not anchored in this kind of early and deeply personal experience.

Kelly's approach, in which the most basic principle is that human beings construct their world, sits easily with the ideas of writers like Berger and Luckmann. As a psychological rather than a sociological account, its essential concern is with understanding what this constructivism actually means for an individual. And in its perspective, the idea of expertise takes on a very different character from the one we conventionally give it. If people construct what they know through their engagements in the social world, then we must necessarily see each person's 'body of knowledge' as, in some sense, unique. Your expertise then becomes, not the possession of a standard package of material acquired from others at second hand, but your own intricate personal landscape through which you are free to move at will from one interesting vista to another.

As Berger and Luckmann suggest, our understanding of the world, of our own human realities, exists at different levels. What we most deeply know, what we feel in our bones to be true, represents a different order of knowledge from, say, the technicalities of the Dutch grammar we are now teaching ourselves. It is perhaps the relation between these two levels of understanding which is, above all, the concern of Kellyan psychology. The relation of explicit knowledge to deeper levels of understanding is not standard. It is possible, for instance, to have quite an elaborate system of knowledge about some area which has only slight personal significance. Because you can only afford to run an old banger, you have had of necessity to learn a lot about motor mechanics; but the understanding is only instrumental. You can talk as well as anyone about big ends and blowing gaskets, but you really find the topic of cars extremely boring. It cannot compare with the personal investment, the emotional depth, of your interest in music. From this point of view, the degree to which an area of understanding touches the deepest, most personal roots of what we know represents our real commitment to it.

The interrelation of different kinds of knowledge may, however, be more complicated. The women maths teachers studied by Walden and Walkerdine experienced their situation as anomalous because of what were essentially contradictions in what they knew. The explicit understanding they expressed as maths teachers could not sit easily with the deep understanding they possessed as women. Because what we know is, ultimately, what we know about ourselves, these women, within our particular society, were having to struggle with two apparently incompatible kinds of knowledge. In a sense, they lacked integrity – the harmony between our conscious verbalized knowledge and what, in our bones, we really know to be true.

How does all this appear if we apply it broadly to teaching? What it suggests most of all, perhaps, is an alternative perspective on the differences between teachers. Traditionally, teachers have been seen as good or bad, as competent or incompetent, as more or less effective. This implies an essential commonality of aim, of material; it views teachers as all trying to do the same thing, and doing it well or not so well. But if knowledge is essentially a construction, a construction which ramifies into what is deeply personal, into the inarticulate as well as the explicit, then, in teaching, every teacher is doing something unique. When we teach, we do, in a sense, teach ourselves. As teachers, we do not just act as the gateway to knowledge. We ourselves represent, embody, our curriculum. And, in our teaching, we convey not just our explicit knowledge, but also our position towards it, the personal ramifications and implications which it has for us. If we look at teaching like this, it does not seem so much a matter of teaching more or less well, but more a question of *what* is being taught. The boredom, the bad faith, the inner doubts towards the material – all this comes over just as much as the sense of richness, excitement, possibility that it evokes. Some teachers teach their own positive stance towards the curriculum they have constructed. Others, who stand in part estranged from what they teach, communicate unclear, complicated messages, secret reservations, personal separation, an inner discomfort with the content they explicitly put over.

Teachers as teachers of themselves; that is one view which a Kellyan psychology seems to invite. However, teachers are also teachers of children, and, from a Kellyan viewpoint, teaching entails not just a personal stance towards constructed knowledge, but also a personal stance towards the children being taught. In their experience of classroom work, teachers are essentially experiencing an engagement with children or adolescents. And how they stand towards the young is, of course, absolutely vital in governing the kind of teaching they do. This, too, is a matter of personal construction – of the meanings with which youth and childishness have come to be invested. One aspect of these meanings arises out of the positions of adults towards the children they themselves were, the child who is still somewhere within them. To people whose childhood experiences remain accessible to them, sources of interest, reflection, pleasure, the presence of children is enjoyable, and engagement with them can be lively and meaningful. For other adults, whose childhoods are not like this, their childish selves are felt to be alien, embarrassing, even repugnant, not fitting with the adult self they have constructed for themselves. To people like this, the childish identities of others are essentially uncomfortable, and can be tolerated only by being strictly channelled within adult modes.

On this logic, the intercourse between teachers and children is itself constructed out of the position which each takes towards the other. And, obviously, no teacher adopts identical positions towards every child within the class. In the study of teachers and teaching, there is, of course, a long tradition of work which focuses on particular differentiated relations between teachers and their pupils. Much of this has followed from the implications of the much publicized study by Rosenthal and Jacobsen (1968). This study argued that teachers, by their own expectations, tended to create the very differences in educational attainment which they anticipated between middle-class and working-class children. Despite the criticisms levelled at this study, later work, summarized by Brophy and Good (1974), substantially confirmed the importance of teachers' expectations. In any new class some children will speak less 'correctly', look less prepossessing, scruffier than others. For many a teacher, they are the ones from whom rather less can be expected. And, lo and behold, after a year in the class, relative levels of attainment in classwork bear out just this prediction. Yet, in a neighbouring classroom where the teacher does not see children in these terms, no such differences appear. More recently, work of this kind has begun to look at how teachers see the meaning of gender, and of ethnic and cultural differences, and thereby sometimes inadvertently bring about the educational disadvantages they expect in girls or black pupils. An example of such unconscious stereotyping of black pupils is described by E. M. Brittain (1976). It will be important, in Chapter 7 concerned with classroom relationships, to look in more detail at the way in which these things actually happen. For the moment, they serve to illustrate the idea that teachers take particular stances towards the children they teach.

If we take seriously the idea that, in teaching, an adult adopts a personal stance towards the children in the classroom, this means thinking about what teaching particular kinds of pupil may really involve. The position of a teacher towards a heterogeneous group of pupils entails more than just a natural liking for some, an antipathy towards others, a sense of congeniality or strangeness, of relative involvement or distance in relation to particular pupils. In teaching, we are essentially inviting children to take up, at least provisionally, our own personal stance towards the curriculum. That invitation can be credibly made only to those whom we ourselves can really envisage taking it up. If white, male, middle-class teachers have typically been found, in research studies, to produce their best results with white, male middle-class pupils, that is not really surprising. Nor that, when a black teacher is appointed, she does wonders for the black children in her class. As a black woman, that teacher knows a great deal about the personal world of her black pupils, especially the girls. For her, the journey they could make, the position they could take up, in order to adopt something of her own stance to the curriculum, is already clear. She knows that they could make that journey, that it would be meaningful to them, and that in making it, they would not need to leave behind all that is personally valid in their lives. She believes in the possibility, and the fertility, of this learning for this group of pupils. All this presupposes such a teacher to stand confident and four square, in her teaching role. Alone among her white colleagues, were she to doubt her own position, to feel a sense of self-mistrust, her impact on her black pupils might be as negative as that of the Walden and Walkerdine women maths teachers.

This is one way of looking at the self-fulfilling prophecy, whereby teachers unwittingly produce the educational differences they expect between different pupils. We all find it much easier to imagine the situation of other people whose lives are like our own. As teachers, we know what it would mean for children who are like our own earlier selves to become interested in the curriculum we are offering them. We know they *could* become involved in it, and we can sense what *sort* of involvement they could develop. It is this sense, indeed, which allows us to introduce our material to pupils in their own terms, in forms that they can grasp and engage with. But for other children in the class, who seem very unlike the children we were ourselves, whose personal lives are mysterious, even alien – what does this curriculum mean to them, what could it mean? Despite our best intentions, and our conscientious efforts to teach them, we cannot really envisage their personal engagement with the material. The invitation we issue remains unreal, hollow; the children cannot take it up. For all its ostensibly positive, enabling character, the message of the teaching is clear: all this is not for you.

Yet gulfs like these are not always unbridgeable. There are on record, and in the experience of many people, some teachers who have succeeded in engaging personally with children whose backgrounds are utterly different from their own. In her unique and extraordinary teaching, Sylvia Ashton-Warner (1963) finally broke through to the Maori children in her charge. There were vast differences between her world and theirs: the world of a white middle-class New Zealand woman, and the grossly impoverished, violent world of the Maori subculture. Yet, in daring to 'hear' these children, to relate personally to them, Ashton-Warner managed to grasp something of their real experience. It was, in the end, her affirmation of this experience, by making it the curriculum of her teaching, which proved the turning point in the children's learning to read. Where, in our society, teachers have been able to bridge the gulfs of race, class or gender, and to meet children who are very different from themselves, it has been through a very personal entering into those children's worlds. Only through lived personal experience is it possible to learn something of the situation of strangers.

One aspect of the position which, in teaching, teachers take towards children has to do with the institution of schooling itself. As a teacher you do, of course, necessarily adopt a positive stance towards schooling. You represent an affirmation of school learning, of the legitimacy and value of the teacher's role. You implicitly endorse the system whereby knowledge is constructed and certified in schools. One visible index of all this is the authority you hold in the classroom as the teacher. And this authority is inescapable, it cannot be wished away. Try as you will to establish classroom democracy, to insist on your first name, to be just an informal friend to the children, for those children you remain Miss, the teacher, in charge. For many people, the stance of teaching is a complicated one. The position of teacher may sit oddly with other positions they have held, or still hold. For example, as a child you were known as a bad pupil, always at odds with school and teachers. However, these seemingly contradictory stances, if they can be integrated, may lead in the end to unusual kinds of insight. In her success in relating to her Maori pupils, Sylvia Ashton-Warner may have been helped by the fact that, like them, she was herself an outsider, viewed by her professional colleagues with disapproval, even distaste. Others, like Postman and Weingartner (1969), have shown the fruitfulness of an apparently paradoxical stance in enabling teaching to be, not the automatic endorsement of the status quo, but essentially a 'subversive activity'.

A Kellyan view of teaching and teachers is, clearly, very different from the one we usually take. Its assumptions stand in contrast to many of the assumptions that are built into initial or in-service training. One way of summing up its essential differences from both the other views we have looked at is to see all three approaches as having distinctive focuses. The skills approach ultimately makes teaching a matter of *how*, where the Rogerian one makes it a question of *who*. Neither approach has much to say about *what*. For a personal construct psychology, what is taught has crucial importance, but both the content and the way in which it is offered are part of the person of the teacher. That person, in Kelly's definition, is much more elaborated than the person in Rogers's philosophy. Taking a Kellyan view of teachers as people and teaching as personal, we can, perhaps, gain a wider and more interesting perspective on the classroom landscape.

3 Children's school stances

I spent that first day picking holes in paper, then went home in a
smouldering temper.
'What's the matter, Love? Didn't he like it at school then?'
'They never gave me the present.'
'Present? What present?'
'They said they'd give me a present.'
'Well, now, I am sure they didn't.'
'They did. They said, 'You're Laurie Lee, aren't you? Well, just you
sit there for the present.' I sat there all day, but I never got it. I
ain't going back there again (Lee 1965).

This sad little story is often quoted. Evidently, Laurie Lee's
experience speaks to many people of their own. As they enter
the door for their first day at school, probably most children
look and feel ignorant and foolish. Yet, by the age of 5, any
child is highly knowledgeable, and has acquired a huge range
of personal understanding. How is it that schools, set up with
the best possible intentions, staffed by people who have children's interests at heart, so often fail to meet the child half-
way, to engage with children on their own terms?

In Kellyan psychology, we are defined by the understandings
we have constructed, the world of meanings we deal in, and
inhabit. These understandings, these meanings, are not transmit-
ted to us; we create them ourselves, through our engagements
with the world. They are inseparable from our experience
– the positions we have taken, the choices we have made, the
undertakings we have launched. The knowledge of 5-year-old
children cannot be divorced from their participation in life.

A few years ago, Barbara Tizard and Martin Hughes (1984)
studied thirty 4-year-old girls, comparing the mornings they
spent at nursery school with their afternoons at home. Since
the focus of the study was talk, these little girls' conversations
were all tape-recorded, through small microphones sewn into
their clothes. Tizard and Hughes were therefore able to make
detailed comparisons of the children's talk with their nursery

school teachers, and the conversations they had at home with their mothers. The comparisons yielded startling contrasts.

From their talk at home, these little girls emerge as 'persistently questioning, puzzling minds', constantly demonstrating a lively intellectual curiosity. As they strive to understand a new word, grasp an unfamiliar idea, or fit new information into what they already know, the children are clearly searching, making strenuous efforts in their urgent quest for further knowledge. All this is very different from the way they appear in the nursery school context. They are subdued and passive towards adults, rather than spontaneous in conversation. Exchanges with teachers are typically short-lived and monosyllabic, consisting of minimal responses to the questions put to them. The tone of these exchanges is usually very low key and flat, in contrast with the liveliness typical of their conversations at home. Like Laurie Lee on his first day at school, these little girls appear far more intellectually limited than, at home, they show themselves to be:

Biologically intact children all master the basic verbal thinking skills. We suspect, therefore, that the children who are said to enter school hardly able to talk are almost always children who can talk perfectly well at home (Tizard and Hughes 1984, p. 160).

On the face of it, this situation is paradoxical. Nursery schools, after all, are designed to be intellectually stimulating. Relative to most home settings in this study, they are extremely well furnished, and well equipped with large- and small-scale play materials. Unlike mothers, nursery school teachers do not have to make room for their children amidst multiple domestic and family responsibilities. Though child numbers are much larger, teachers' attention, and its educational purpose, are undivided.

As most nursery school teachers would readily acknowledge, inquiry is the impetus to understanding. We construct our world in the interrogations we make of it, the questions we put to it. In Tizard and Hughes' study, questions represent a major focus. The girls constantly, persistently, urgently interrogate their mothers at home. Yet, in their nursery school setting, these same children apparently find nothing to ask of their teachers; instead it is the teachers who question them. And whereas, in their own questioning, the children launch long, often complex conversational exchanges, the teachers' questioning typically fails to take off, falls flat. These questions do not lead to learning: it seems that we can develop our understanding only through our *own* inquiries, we cannot undertake new ventures within the terms of another's initiative.

When people ask questions, they put particular aspects of their experience at issue. Tizard and Hughes, in their analysis, looked at the content, the subject matter, of children's questions. As they chat with their mothers – going about the ordinary business of domestic work, feeding or changing the baby, or over a meal – these little girls are typically preoccupied with some aspect of their everyday lives. It is to family relationships, household affairs – the social world they live in and know about – that their questions are addressed. Located within the children's own daily lives, these questions presuppose a shared social experience; and it is just this shared experience which makes them, as inquiries, generally so fertile. What is shared, between questioner and questioned, covers wide spans of time and space. Little children and their mothers both know many places, and can make links across them. Both intimately share past as well as present time; both have a lively anticipation of a shared future.

All this is very different from what is generally involved in the questions nursery school teachers put to their charges. In the Tizard and Hughes study, such inquiries typically centre on the child's use of play materials. Interpreting her task in broadly Piagetian terms, the teacher seeks to develop intellectual understanding by interrogating the child about colour, number, volume or causal relationships. The scope of such questions is necessarily very limited. They are located in the here and now. It is difficult for the teacher to make reference to the habitual activities, interests or involvements of individual children. Her questions are typically addressed, within a relatively impersonal context, to a generalized child, not to a particular participant within a shared social order.

If children acquire, with eagerness and intensity, a rich array of understanding about the social world of home, it is because in that world they are themselves active agents. Even in the early years of life, children have their part to play in the family scene. They are involved as participants in what happens, not merely spectators of events. As human beings, of a particular age and gender, a particular position in the family, with particular personal characteristics, all children, however young, have to create their own distinctive ways of taking part in the life of their household. They have, as members of that household, to negotiate their own commitments, expectations, responsibilities. There is nothing trivial about all this; small children do not just play at living. What they do, how they conduct themselves, is of real consequence to themselves and those around them. Their knowledge of their own social world is the outcome of their serious engagement in it.

The learning curriculum of school is, of course, connected in a number of ways with children's out-of-school experience. But paradoxically, the same material which, in the classroom, so often passes children by, may become rooted in their real personal understanding through their own life engagements. This is apparent in the results of a recent study by Gustav Jahoda (1983). Jahoda set out to compare the level of understanding of elementary economics of 9-year-old British children and 9-year-olds living in the city of Harare in Zimbabwe. Setting up a mock shop, he questioned the children about prices, profit margins and so on. Very different levels of understanding emerged between the two groups. Trying to explain how shops work, the British children were typically at sea. Most thought that shopkeepers buy goods at their selling price. Even those who understood price differentials still thought that any profits made would be put to shopkeepers' purely personal use. By contrast, most Harare children had not only mastered the concept of profit; they understood that earnings needed to be set aside for the purchase of further goods.

The essential difference between these two groups lies in the context of their learning. Whereas few British children have direct personal experience of shopkeepers' buying and selling, Harare children typically participate in their parents' small trading. Despite their considerably more sophisticated schooling, British children lag far behind those of urban Zimbabwe in understanding the financial transactions of shopping and trading – transactions that form part, in different ways, of both their worlds. It is evidently through direct involvement, personal engagement, in such transactions that children come to assimilate what they entail. In this they achieve a grasp of principles, not through any formal or explicit teaching, but through their own participation in the social negotiations which actually constitute these principles.

The idea that children learn through their own activity is, of course, not new. It represents the central building-block of the whole Piagetian edifice, and, as such, has exercised great influence on the organization of learning in school, particularly at primary level. Yet, as Margaret Donaldson has shown (1978), it is not enough to provide children with opportunities for experimentation; we need to pay attention to the context of these experiments. From Donaldson's own work, it is clear, for instance, that a 6-year-old apparently unable to conserve volume in the traditional Piagetian test, is perfectly well able to do so if the task involves chocolate to be shared between herself and another child. As Donaldson puts it, young children think in human, not in abstract terms. If we want to assess their level of intellectual understanding, we must do so through questions that are embedded in familiar contexts and activities, that make human rather than merely formal sense. Only later, when such embedded thinking has been thoroughly mastered, will it be possible to progress to abstract principles and formal, logical thought.

It seems likely that, in many nursery schools and reception classes, teachers would define their teaching in just these terms. Typically, much care is exercised, in setting up young children's first encounters with the school world, to make that world as *homely* as possible. The furnishings of the classroom are informal, comfortable, cosy. The activities offered are essentially familiar rather than strange, with play being the major mode. The position of teachers towards their small charges is not far removed from a maternal role, involving support and care-giving at least as much as instruction. In all this, early school experience would be seen as an extension of home experience, rather than a departure from it. The intellectual development expected would be very much within the context of the child's familiar world. The tasks, the activities, would be human ones, embedded in what is already known.

These early school contexts seem at first sight to represent a real continuation of young children's lives at home – to start from where the child is. Yet, looked at more closely, certain critical differences appear. Tizard and Hughes, in the study just described, noted that the nursery school settings, in their furnishings, their books and toys, approximated much more closely to the homes of some girls than those of others. There were clear disjunctions, for certain children, between what was permitted or encouraged in the home and school – getting paint on the floor, for instance. In the case of some girls, the priorities of the two worlds were very different; the high value set on freedom of expression in school, for example, running counter to the importance, for mothers, of strictly kept behavioural norms. In all this, social class did, of course, play an important role.

If the social world of school can often sit uncomfortably with the social world of working-class families, the misfit is obviously more likely when it comes to the situation of those who are not indigenous white children. As Brian Jackson (1979) has shown, there can sometimes be a total lack of engagement between such children and the teachers they encounter on arrival at school. In a small-scale, close-up study, Jackson chose to focus on six northern English children, all living in the same street but with very different cultural backgrounds. Each child was about to start school, and Jackson, having got to know them at home, followed them there. Here is his description of one child's entry:

Yasmin enters school with a push. Her eight-year-old brother, Mohammed, propels her with his hand in the small of her back. Through the green doors and stop. Then like an intense little shunting engine he thrusts her in two-yard spurts along the corridor. 'This is my sister Yasmin, she is quite good', he said masterfully. 'Go to my class now', and abruptly he was off down the corridor and through door and over yard to his own class of Juniors.

Yasmin has thick black curly hair, large brown eyes and a set face that might – if you know her – be patient or bewildered or plain blank. She is dressed beautifully, as if for a party: a fresh green tunic, close-fitting green trousers – half-way between *shalwar* and children's drainpipes. Round her waist, a broad black belt, with a huge sparkling diamante fastening. And oddly, short black wellington boots.

She said nothing. It was difficult for the teachers to establish whether she spoke or understood English at all, whether she expected to stay to school dinner or even how old she was (Jackson 1979, p. 25).

Of the six children observed by Jackson, only one, Victoria, had been born to a white indigenous family.

In the first week [the teacher] is not really picking out the children individually. Victoria has forced herself on her attention. So have several similar children. There is a confidence in their classroom exchanges. [The teacher] is fairly sure about Noel too: when the headmistress comes in she often speaks to Noel – after all she knows his mother and their take-away shop. Yasmin and Angelica are, this first week, rather like two beautiful dolls: and not the living complex character that Victoria clearly announces that *she* is. Gopal and Beauregard are much more part of the background: wary, obedient, not proferring relationship. . . . These are probably the two children who need the most delicate reception (ibid., p. 99).

In the Tizard and Hughes study, it was working-class children who, relative to those with middle-class backgrounds, stood at a disadvantage. But, as Jackson argues, the situation of Victoria, alone among these six new entrants to schooling, is, at least potentially, accessible to the many primary school teachers whose own background is upper working or lower middle class. Inevitably, things go worse with children whose identity and lifestyle is framed by other cultures altogether.

The teachers simply do not know about the children's homes, backgrounds, pre-school years. With three of the children, even their names in the class register are doubtful. Yasmin and Gopal are recorded in bastardized Western forms ('But what is your *Christian* name, dear?' I several times heard teachers say to Islamic, Hindu or Sikh children) and Chuc Win is known only by his adopted name. . . . Because the teacher is not inward with the child's life-style, the child actually doesn't make sense in school (ibid., p. 136).

Jackson's study vividly documents the gulf that can exist in what is offered and received between schools and pupils who are not from the cultural mainstream. Just as Yasmin was clearly at sea in the classroom world where her older brother dumped her, so her teacher was equally unable to recognize, to meet, the expectations, interests, engagements which Yasmin brought to school. There is, of course, no way of bridging this huge cultural divide, without a social commitment, as Jackson puts it, to 'eliciting cultural positives and extending cultural dialogue within education'. A major part of this, obviously, involves reworking professional teacher training, not merely to incorporate a multicultural element, but to systematically broaden the cultural base within which teaching and learning are defined.

If we are to do justice to all minority groups in our

multicultural society, we need to give far greater acknowledgement to the experience and lifestyle of children such as Yasmin
or Gopal. This is not just a matter of ensuring that wider
recognition is offered to alternative cultural *contexts*. We have
to recognize that cultural membership entails acting as a parti-
cularized social *agent*. As participants in their own distinctive
worlds of family and neighbourhood, Yasmin, Noel and Beauregard play their part in the life they share with others. Each
represents a particular way of engaging with the world, a
particular stance.

To see children as social agents has many implications. Some
of these have to do with power. As agents in our social world,
we must all negotiate politically with each other. Some of the
most intellectually developing conversations, in the Tizard and
Hughes study, take place when their 4-year-old subjects are in
conflict with their mothers. In disputing, challenging maternal
limits and strictures, these girls have of necessity to find
reasons, meet arguments, produce justifications, explicate their
thinking. The learning this involves, though often painful, is
certainly real. It has to do with the limits and possibilities of
their own lived engagements.

Conflicts also arise in the world of school; by the fourth year
at secondary level there is typically a loud chorus of protesting
voices. Teachers, the curriculum, rules and regulations, the
whole schooling regime are the object of open resentment, if
not actual rebellion, among many young people who are
obliged to attend school. Teachers themselves are necessarily
much concerned with containing and managing this kind of
reaction. Yet, in the way we typically view it, we draw a
clear dividing line between political protest and educational
development. The first, we believe, has to do with order,
discipline. The problems are problems within the social *context*
of learning; the essence of learning itself lies in another realm
altogether – that of the official curriculum of education.

But this disjunction cannot really hold. In Kelly's terms, it is
through our behaviour that we ask questions: personal conduct
represents a testing out of possibilities. The adolescent student,
whose persistent answering back to a tired and exasperated
teacher finally results in his exclusion from the lesson, is
engaged in learning which is personal and real. Through his
own enactment, his actual participation in events, he produces
an outcome which has personal significance for him. This

learning is learning about his own position, about the meaning of the stance he is taking towards school. It comes about, not through his reception, as pupil, of an official curriculum, but through his own active engagement as a participant in social events.

It is this kind of perspective on learning which has informed work on 'the hidden curriculum' of school. As Basil Bernstein (1982) and others have shown, the fundamental lessons of schooling may be of a very different order from its explicit aims. Most basically, in going to school, children learn their social place. The hierarchy of school is not just an academic one. In a society which is racist, sexist, and classist, children find their own position within the social order of school – a social order which, inevitably, carries something of these divisions.

We all learn through our own engagement with events. Children do not acquire the social understandings embodied in the hidden curriculum merely through being exposed to school. Young people involve themselves in their own school lives; they position themselves towards others in their school contexts. If children learn that their place, within these contexts, is structured by their gender or their social class, this is because they themselves actually operate, in their social transactions with teachers and with each other, in terms of these dimensions. That this is so, even in the earliest years of school, can be seen from the work of Walden and Walkerdine (1985). Here are their comments on the play which they observed among three nursery school children:

Although the results of our study show that children are not very sure of what gender means in its wider connotations, they are able to divide those closest to them, peers, family, teachers etc into the right categories. And more than that, they are aware . . . of what being a certain gender means in terms of what behaviour can be expected of them. They are able to manipulate the social relations in different ways within the framework they have set up. . . . Nancy is able to manipulate herself into a position of power and dominance. . . . Although its focus may be imaginary, play is rarely nonsensical, it is firmly rooted in existing and everyday social relations. The children create a microcosm of the world outside. Diane as 'mother' implies someone who has not only to tidy up but who should be obeyed, and the game finishes when Nancy

refuses to accept this any longer and goes off to something else
(pp. 34–5).

All this suggests that we should take seriously the social
learning which goes on in schools, and that we should view
young learners as learning by virtue of their own social engagements. We must then necessarily concern ourselves with the
particular kind of social position which children come to take
up *as school pupils*. For the unkindest critics of this fundamental
aspect of the hidden curriculum, what children learn in their
earliest days at school is that they must now inhabit a world
where tasks are meaningless and talk bizarre. The activities of
the classroom seem unconnected with any of the real purposes
of life: 'busyness' is all. The discourse of school is after all, in
human terms, very strange. As pupil, you must bid for your
right to speak at all, and when you do, you must speak only
of particular things, in particular ways. You have to learn,
through questioning that is full of traps, to produce the 'right'
answer for an adult who already knows it.

Although this picture is, of course, a caricature, there are
nevertheless certain distinctive features of life in school which
children must necessarily absorb if they are to function in it.
The text which young children must learn, in order to become
school pupils, has been the focus of study for Mary Willes
(1983). She argues that, to make the necessary transition, children need to learn the particular rules of discourse that define
communication within the classroom world. From this viewpoint, what is critical is the acquisition of certain 'good
manners', a particular kind of 'etiquette' which operates in
school life. And the importance of etiquette in governing how
young children come to be defined as pupils, is certainly borne
out by work such as that carried out by Rachel Sharp and Tony
Green (1976).

The progressive primary school which formed the subject of
Sharp and Green's study was informal and non-authoritarian.
Yet despite this, the children who entered its gates came early
to be differentiated, in terms which carried their own clear
educational prognoses.

As the children enter the class, the teacher attempts to develop
working categories for her relationship with them. These
categories have implications for their likely success, failure,

difficulties and so on. There may be some 'form' on the child, or its family background which will influence the initial stance of the teacher. . . . Karen had 'form' – she had an older brother in the school who had proved troublesome, and there was friction between the parents and the school. . . . Karen's behaviour did fit the preconceptions. She was defined as being 'noisy' and 'raucous'. . . . She tended to push in and shout, or make her requests to the teacher in a loud voice. As the teacher observed, the child did not say 'Excuse me, Mrs ———' she did not know how to approach people. Thus it was mainly on the grounds of poor etiquette that the teacher had transformed the background expectation into a practical observation and an attitude to the child (Sharp and Green 1976, p. 140).

Under the apparently simple idea of etiquette lie many complexities and subtleties. How young children stand towards their reception class teacher is not adequately understood by saying that they have learned, or failed to learn, certain standard rules of discourse. Such terms act to disguise the fact that, in communication with teachers, social relations – *differentiated* social relations – are involved. Children start school as particular social agents, who have already come to adopt certain characteristic positions towards others in the social world. The demands of school may entail postures that seem altogether incomprehensible, or irreconcilable with familiar lived positions. The vital social learning of early schooling may be baffling or painful. It is not so much a matter of acquiring a new kind of etiquette, as of coming to take up a particular kind of stance towards school. For some new school entrants, the stance they adopt will allow an engagement with the educational curriculum. For others, it will not. And, for the second case, one does not need to be a Yasmin or a Beauregard.

For one girl, the world of school is happily continuous with the world of home. Each world is familiar with the other. Her role and identity across the two are consonant, integral. She finds herself known, acknowledged, affirmed by teachers – people who are not so different from her parents and their circle. Her relationships with her own friends in school echo and endorse her positive stance towards the business of schooling. For this girl to engage herself personally with the activities of lessons, to enter into conversation with teachers about the material they present – this sits happily with the sense she has made of her life so far, the positions she habitually takes up within her social world.

There is another girl in the class group for whom things are very different. In the pupil role that is offered by school, she cannot recognize the person she is outside its gates. The two realms are mutually strange, cannot achieve any real communication with each other. The world which knows and respects her is not there in the official business of the classroom. Only through her engagements with peers, it seems, can this world be sustained and represented. In a school which channels and closely monitors the social encounters of pupils, increasingly these engagements come, perhaps, to be defined as deviant, resisting the real purposes of education. As time goes on, this girl may find herself adopting a stance which is *against* official schooling. Those who do well in the classroom, who get on with the teachers, who are in the exam set, are on the other side – brain boxes, snobs, posh people. Her own mates, like herself, take up an oppositional position towards the material, and the agents, of classroom work. To do otherwise, at this stage, would be to sell out, to compromise themselves. For this girl, the possibilities of a less alienated stance must depend upon an exceptionally delicate kind of communication on the part of teachers. Only if her vital engagements, her identity as a particular social participant can be understood, appreciated, respected, is there a hope of reconciling her lived position with an involvement in school learning. Those teachers who, for instance, sometimes integrate peer group relations with classroom activities, in collaborative modes of learning, demonstrate that there are possibilities for bridging gulfs such as these.

Schooling is not adequately defined as only its official curriculum. But nor is it enough just to note that a hidden curriculum exists, whereby the divisions of society become reproduced. Schools are not, of course, a world apart. Teachers cannot, of themselves, act to prevent the power structure of the wider society informing the social order of school. Yet we must acknowledge that that social order is actively created through the lived engagements of school life in and out of the classroom. In this, even the youngest pupils are already particular social agents. If the essentially active, participatory character of social learning can be recognized, made explicit, talked about in school, possibilities may arise for reworking something of its social order, for acknowledging and perhaps beginning to change the alienated stance of some school pupils.

4   Personal education

Learning is inescapably personal. Each of us, in living, is engaged in constructing the meaning of our lives. The interpretations we make of ourselves and our world, although they have their currency in our dealings with others, are uniquely ours. Just as the knowledge that every teacher offers is essentially personal, has its own distinctive ramifications, so, in learning, pupils construct an understanding which is theirs alone. For one girl in the second year design and technology class, working on her model bridge means the confirmation of her feminine incompetence in operating equipment. For the boy working nearby, the lesson has quite another meaning, connected with his sense of closeness to his car mechanic father and the reaction he expects when he demonstrates the completed bridge at home that evening.

The definition of learning as personal is something of a truism in most accounts of education. Yet, if we examine it closely this definition sits oddly with many of the ways in which schooling is organized. In 1969 Edward Blishen compiled a book from essays on school by secondary school children for a competition organized by the *Observer*. Through these pupils' comments runs, as a major theme, their sense of personal separation from formal education. Expressed as wistful longing or angry resentment, this sense of exclusion arises out of the small, as well as the larger features of life at secondary school. Although these comments were made in 1969, they seem to speak equally for today's secondary school children.

In their judgements of their own educational experience, Blishen's young people describe their schooling as often entailing a disrespect for personal individuality. Being a pupil means being herded in large groups by the relentless clanging of bells. Regardless of what you are doing at that moment, how deeply involved you may be in your work, you must instantly cut off and switch to another lesson, another teacher, another wavelength. You have your being, as school pupil, in places that are physically uncomfortable, highly public, and lacking any stamp of personal expression. Nor can you express yourself in your own person, which often has to be standardized by school uniform, without your own style and adornments. Throughout the school day you are subject to rules and prohibitions; there is little scope for personal choice, individual initiative.

As Blishen comments, when structures and timetables are rigid, they act to eliminate any really personal contact with teachers, who become 'aloof, authoritative people, instead of ordinary companionable human beings'. The curriculum is increasingly dominated by exams, and therefore becomes fraught with pressure, tension and fear, rather than suffused with personal enjoyment. Instead of the 'whole realms of fascinating subjects waiting to enthral you', you must learn subjects that are arbitrarily chopped up and seem to have nothing to do with life. Though you would like, in your education, to learn about living with other people, the learning of classrooms often involves only dreary abstractions. As Judith, aged 14, remarks of her history lessons:

Shattered and flung about like the splinters of a broken jam-jar, how can all this superficial knowledge be gathered into the swelling, fluctuating flow of life which must have been there?

(Blishen 1969, p. 66)

These young people remain totally dissatisfied with the answer that education is to be instrumentally viewed: 'I am not preparing for life, I am alive now.'

In reflecting on their school experience, many of Blishen's pupils look back wistfully at their primary schools, 'the golden land' they once knew. 'As we get older', remarks one pupil, 'our school life gets less and less interesting.' The progression of education is, broadly, a progression away from person-centred learning towards learning that is knowledge-centred. Whereas in the primary classroom, teachers are seen as 'teaching the child'; teachers at the secondary level are defined as 'teaching the subject'. It is, apparently, only the immaturity of younger children which justifies the personal focus. This implies that with the approach of adolescence, personal concerns can be discarded and attention given to understanding that is independent of individual persons.

Underlying this kind of educational progression is a definition of knowledge as constituting a kind of hierarchy. Those areas of understanding which have an undeniably personal character – the expressive as against the instrumental spheres of knowledge – represent the lower levels in the hierarchy. So, in the school curriculum, art, music, drama or dance are subjects with typically lower prestige than maths, chemistry or physics. Just as primary schools, and those who staff them, are, in general, accorded less status than is granted to the secondary sector, so secondary teachers of art or drama stand lower in the status hierarchy than do maths or science teachers.

Person-centred primary education, and personal, expressive areas of the secondary curriculum, are both traditionally seen as constituting the less advanced, less essentially mature forms of human knowledge. Given the nature of western society, it is, perhaps, hardly surprising that these spheres are typically occupied by women. As a classic study (Broverman *et al.* 1970) has shown, the character of maturity in our usual social scripts is that of the adult male; to be a woman is to some extent to be childish. Certainly, women teachers predominate at primary levels, and in the expressive areas of the secondary curriculum. Girls generally excel in primary but not in secondary education; they opt out of science and maths, preferring the 'softer' options. To the extent that this happens, it can be seen as the living out of appropriate educational roles within a society where knowledge is structured by gender.

The highest understandings as impersonal, as unconnected with human particularity – this is the assumption that underpins the official hierarchy of knowledge. Yet, although this assumption is so widely held in our society, it is not the only way to see knowledge, nor, certainly, the way that many teachers would define things. In an analysis of prevailing ideas about intelligence and understanding, Nicholas Emler and Nicholas Heather (1980) set out to show how questionable these ideas are. Western notions about the most important kinds of knowledge – impersonal, scientific, objective – are, they argue, derived from a way of life which is organized around technological and bureaucratic institutions: 'The scientific method, broadly defined, is the embodiment of a set of values which owe their existence . . . to the survival of a particular institutional structure which sustains them.' Our ideas about knowledge are, of course, culturally relative.

Cultural factors have influenced the way we see knowledge, and in other societies they have produced some very different views of human understanding. We all tend, however, to overlook the influence of culture on our own perspective. As Emler and Heather show, this disregard of the way in which knowledge is socially constructed is built into our psychology of intelligence. For instance, although it is generally believed that IQ tests represent measures of 'pure' intelligence, their real starting point has been that of rather narrowly defined success in the schooling system:

Theoretically inspired research . . . reveals explicitly the psychologist's view of the nature of intelligence. Since this research has invariably taken the educationally-oriented tests as its point of departure, the view it reveals is still heavily inclined towards the educational context. It gives particular prominence to skills relating to literacy and numeracy as does the orthodox school curriculum. Broader questions about the nature and function of intellect have received little attention. We still know very little about the capacities people need to function in their everyday environments, what kinds of intellectually-challenging problems these environments routinely pose for them, and what makes people more or less effective in these environments (Emler and Heather 1980, p. 139).

By equating competence with traditional kinds of educational success, our psychology of intellect presupposes that there is only one way of being intelligent. It gives priority to formal educational skills – those that involve abstraction and the manipulation of symbols. One aspect of this involves setting literacy above spoken language:

An established tradition of written transmission of beliefs also has repercussions for the character of knowledge. . . . Knowledge is no longer to be found now in social relations, in dialogue, but in disembodied form by the lone individual. Likewise the production of knowledge becomes an exclusively individual affair. Literacy conspires to divorce learning and discovery from an interpersonal context and places knowledge on an impersonal plane, as a universalized, disinterested, socially detached, and preferably abstract entity (ibid., p. 141).

Just the same valuation of abstract forms of knowledge, so these writers argue, is carried by Piagetian ideas. Intellectual progression, in this logic, means moving further and further away from personally centred kinds of understanding towards thought that is independent of particular human contexts, and centred in logical and mathematical structures. In its content, mature thought is defined as unrelated to the social world, and concerned instead with 'the categories of knowledge that preoccupy physicists and natural philosophers: space, time causality, substance and number' (ibid., p. 144).

In all this, academic ideas about intelligence and cognitive development both support and are supported by certain traditional assumptions about education. These assumptions value technical rather than social skills, and set abstract and impersonal kinds of understanding above knowledge which is grounded in human concerns and personal contexts. The progression from primary to secondary schooling is a move from person-centred to subject-centred learning. The hierarchy of school subjects reserves the highest status for forms of knowledge that are essentially depersonalized. Yet, as teachers themselves know well, the personal cannot be kept out of education; it persists in intruding into classroom life. However, because of the way we generally conceptualize schooling, we tend to view these personal intrusions as problematic. Just as the protests, the resistance, of adolescents in school are typically seen in 'discipline' rather than in 'learning' terms, so, when encounters with pupils are undeniably personal, we often characterize them in a special kind of language – a language that is distinct from the one we use to describe educational progress.

From the standpoint of Kellyan psychology, human learning is necessarily a personal affair, arising out of particular kinds of human inquiry, and rooted in particular life contexts. Any discussion of what, or how, children learn, has to accommodate their personal concerns, their human realities, their positions as living participants in a shared social order. Two languages – one for school learning, another for 'personal individuality' – will not do. It is, perhaps, our characteristically divided perspectives on children in school which have brought about some of the difficulty and confusion in regard to pupils with 'special needs'.

The legal requirement on schools to 'implement Warnock'[1] has resulted in much consciousness-raising and many training courses, as well as a proliferation of literature concerned with special needs. Integration has, of course, been seen as the crucial issue. How far can the limits of schools be pushed out to accommodate children with very low ability, with specific disabilities, with serious behavioural problems? If certain pupils prove impossible to contain, what kind of special facilities should be set up for their education? Are the advantages of segregated units – with their specialized, dedicated staff, their curricular freedom, their personal continuity – outweighed by the huge stigma of attending a 'mad school'?

Yet, however large, however urgently, the integration issues loom, other, more fundamental issues lurk behind them. Integrated or not, children with special needs seem to remain problematic. One 'benefit', for instance, that this categorization confers is that of priority admission to preschool nursery education. But, as Patricia Potts (1984) suggests:

It can be argued that the priority system ensures that those who need the provision most get a place. The trouble is that children with special needs who enter on a priority ticket can still be seen as second-class citizens. . . . Identifying groups of children as 'disadvantaged', even if this is a prelude to positive discrimination, can only be socially divisive (p. 5).

As with many such changes of nomenclature, the term 'special needs' was seen as avoiding the stigma associated with the labels 'maladjusted', 'ESN' or 'physically handicapped'. Referring to *needs* meant defining children in terms of appropriate educational provision rather than in terms of personal deficiency. Yet, somehow, escape from stigma has not proved so easy. However categorized, these pupils are in 'Catch 22': either set apart in segregated units, or else standing out, all too visibly, in mainstream schools, as 'special', different, other.

There is something paradoxical in the definition of one in every six children as having needs outside the normal scope of 'comprehensive' schools. Yet, as things are, there is no doubt that many pupils in this category do make difficult, perhaps sometimes impossible, demands on ordinary classroom teaching. What are the features that render these children so problematic as school pupils? 'Special needs' are a mixed bag, made up of three different sorts of characteristic. Disabilities such as profound deafness or the mobility disorders of cerebral palsy constitute one category. Very low ability is another. The third is that of behavioural deviance, in the form, for instance, of extreme hyperactivity, or violent aggressiveness.

Children such as these do, obviously, themselves experience difficulties in living; and they present undeniable difficulties for those around them. Yet such difficulties are seldom insurmountable. Educationally, where difficult children have been most fruitfully, most successfully engaged, this has been because the teachers working with them have been able to develop a mutually responsive personal dialogue. In this, the particular identity of the individual child has been recognized, acknowledged, respected. Just as, for the parents of a Downs Syndrome child, their daughter is most distinctively, most uniquely herself, so for the teacher in a special school, the pupils in her charge represent highly differentiated young people, whose human character can in no way be encompassed within the label 'maladjusted'.

For teachers who are able to see difficult children in such personal terms, the educational task becomes that of making the setting and the curriculum responsive to the individual child. It is a question of fitting the educational regime to the pupil, rather than the other way round. And, for many of those with first-hand personal experience of 'special' categorization, the *problem* typically does lie in the educational context rather than in the child.

If cerebral palsied children cannot be accommodated in ordinary schools, this is because these schools have failed to provide lifts and ramps, and have thereby created their own mobility barriers. If some pupils prove impossibly restless in class, this arises out of the routine insistence that lively, physically ebullient young people must sit quietly at their desks for 45 minutes at a stretch. If children of very limited academic ability cannot be fitted into the classroom, this shows that the school's mixed-ability policy needs further elaboration. More broadly, the difficulties which many 'special' pupils experience in school may relate to a setting which seems large, frightening, insensitive, and a curriculum which offers few opportunities for personal engagement. Peter Newell (1983) sees integration as

part of a wider struggle of people with sensory, mental and physical handicaps to gain full access to the ordinary community and its institutions – and so should very often be thought of as concentrating on buildings with special needs rather than people with special needs. It is . . . part of the battle for genuinely comprehensive community schools, which meet the needs, including the special needs, of all those in their area who want to use them (p. 7).

Looked at in this way, the problem of pupils with special needs becomes a problem of the mismatch between schools and those they set out to cater for. And certain educational problems have, in fact, already been redefined. This happened when, through the action of pressure groups within the Afro-Caribbean community, the concepts of *slow learning* and *disruptive* came into sharp focus. These categories, once brought into question, began for many people to take on quite another character. The problematic interface between many black children and school learning, previously defined as individualized difficulties, now came to be seen in different, essentially cultural terms. This redefinition carried implications of the extent to which mainstream cultural values, assumptions and practices are, implicitly, embedded within ordinary classroom life. By the same token, the ascription of 'deviance' was seen, in these categorizations, to embody the norms of particular dominant social groupings, and to act as a smokescreen hiding essentially political issues.

If special needs are looked at as problems *between* school settings and particular children, rather than as problems *within* those children, this has implications for reconsidering, reworking mainstream educational provision. It means something rather different, where the curriculum is involved, than in other, less tangible aspects of school life. Among those who have been striving to make integration an educational reality, there is general agreement that, of the three special needs categories, it is *behavioural* deviance which poses the most serious problems. This is not to say that there are easy solutions to integrating children with specific handicaps or very low ability. In the context of extreme financial stringency, the allocation of limited resources cannot but be problematic. In principle, tutorial help and support could be given in an ordinary classroom to children with serious academic difficulties. Visual aids and sign language interpreters could be brought in for those with sensory deficits. For children whose first language is not English, mother-tongue teaching, and two-way translation of texts and worksheets could be ensured. The curriculum of learning – as much good practice has shown – could, potentially, be comprehensively opened up to accommodate the diversity of interests, backgrounds, and academic levels of any genuinely mixed pupil group. But, for all this to be achieved, would call upon a level of staffing and financial support which simply does not exist. As things are, the commitment of precious resources to these areas of development would necessarily eliminate possibilities of maintaining 'special' facilities – facilities which, in this early stage of integration, no one can afford to discard.

If integration of children with very low ability, or specific handicaps, is seriously constrained by a real dearth of financial and other resources, children with behavioural difficulties pose problems of another order altogether. For disturbed, disruptive children, accommodation in ordinary school settings is far more difficult. Since behavioural 'deviance' tests to the very limit the commitment to truly personal learning, it is important to examine closely the educational problems which such pupils pose. Characteristically, it is not the explicit curriculum of school, but its hidden curriculum, that they call into question. By the way they behave, these children disrupt the whole fabric on which the official business of education rests. They ignore, or they reject, the vital assumptions, values, interpersonal relationships which underpin and legitimate classroom learning – and without which schooling cannot proceed. Behavioural deviance strikes at what is most crucial and least acknowledged in the way we organize education.

It is because we typically view learning in cognitive terms – terms that make little reference to the personal – that our understanding of the hidden curriculum in school remains so limited. Yet if all human behaviour is seen in personal terms, there is no essential separation between learning, on the one hand, and personal transactions, on the other. *Every* act of learning is a kind of personal engagement, and, conversely, every 'refusal' or 'failure' to learn is its own kind of engagement and must be understood within the same perspective. In this approach, problems do not represent a separate, special area of understanding, needing different terms from the ones we used to describe educational processes.

Among the many problems which can arise in classrooms, perhaps that of aggressiveness is the most difficult to contain. A particular boy who is chronically liable to temper tantrums, who constantly attacks and provokes other children, destroys classroom equipment, and is violent to the teacher, is almost bound, eventually, to be excluded. For nearly every teacher, such a child makes classroom life intolerable. There seems no way to get through to him, no possibility of breaking into the vicious circle of escalating violence. The aggressiveness comes apparently unprovoked, out of the blue; and therefore cannot be forestalled. In the end, the boy's behaviour seems inexplicable; he can only be seen as an aggressive, hostile personality. Whatever happens to this boy, whatever special educational provision is offered, it may be that he will never be seen in any other way. Or he may be lucky enough at some stage to encounter a teacher with the persistence and imaginative power to enter into the world he lives in – the world against which he must constantly make his angry protests.

As Kelly suggests, the concept of hostility is ultimately not a helpful one. For as long as we view a child as hostile, we can only write off his actions as bad, unjustified behaviour; we focus, not on what he is trying to say, but on the painful consequences for others of what he is doing. Yet, if we try to see things from his point of view, we may find a way of engaging with him, of entering into a relationship that is not one of mutual angry confrontation. Essentially, hostile behaviour represents a desperate effort to save something that seems about to be irrevocably lost. It is an attempt to cook the books, to deny the evidence that an endeavour has failed. To a 5-year-old boy who needs to win in every game, losing is simply intolerable. If he smashes up equipment, bashes the other players, then perhaps he can come out on top, make them all afraid of him, prove himself the greatest.

For a teacher who views the pupil's hostility like this, his behaviour, though unacceptable, is nevertheless comprehensible. Such a perspective allows the boy to remain within the realm of understandable human action. It becomes possible to engage with his behaviour, rather than simply to dismiss it as pathological. Working with this boy will, necessarily, entail a long and difficult negotiation if he is, in the end, to define his place in the social world in terms other than those of dominance and submission. The negotiation may, ultimately, be unsuccessful; school, after all, is not the only social arena in which the boy participates. But this view of his behaviour does at least allow the possibility of dialogue.

Situations like these are, fortunately, relatively rare in school life. Yet ordinary classroom learning is probably much more often a source of pain than we actually acknowledge. For a 14-year-old pupil starting her option in social studies, the new demands may be profoundly uncomfortable, unsettling. Used to an educational currency of factual knowledge, of written responses to questions, she now finds herself called upon to talk in class, to draw on personal experience, to make her own judgements in spheres that seem to have no right and wrong answers. This new ground is totally bewildering. She does not know where she is, cannot get a clear sense of what the curriculum means, of how, or whether, she should engage herself with the lesson.

By its nature, real learning necessarily entails some measure of discomfort. If we are to shift our position towards things, we must endure feeling for a time at a loss, disoriented, grasping for some new way of understanding what now seems unfamiliar and incomprehensible. The curriculum of education can also make its own contribution to the painfulness of school learning. For all that many teachers have begun to rework their texts and materials, the formal curriculum they are obliged to teach remains broadly monocultural. Although education is supposed to mean access to the whole human heritage, the heritage offered belongs differentially to the members of any classroom group. In the learning they are asked to undertake in school, many children still find no reference to their own cultural background, community life, family patterns. The silence, within the official curriculum, as to the endeavours, the achievements, the social movements of 'their' people contains an implicit denial or marginalization of their own experience and identity. Even for those children whose culture is central to the official curriculum, school learning entails painful possibilities. The story of civilization is, after all, not just a story of heroism. To possess our cultural heritage means coming to terms with a human world which, for all its courage, compassion, imagination, is also everywhere scarred by oppression, hatred, cruelty and betrayal.

In the conventional view of school learners, a few children are picked out as 'special' by reason of their deviance. The rest, it is assumed, can be viewed as broadly uniform. Yet all learning is learning by individuals. When children acquire new knowledge, they take up a way of understanding things that has its unique meaning, its connotations and ramifications into a personal life which is their own. Part of the process of entering into such knowledge entails feeling. Traditionally, we relegate feelings to the sidelines, viewing them, at best, as a by-product, and, at worst, as defining the pathological character of deviant pupils. Yet, so far from being incidental, the presence of emotion in learning is an index of its meaningfulness.

A Kellyan account entails a distinctive perspective on learning as personal. If we take this perspective, we can only endorse the protests of Blishen's young essayists, that it is the impersonality of schooling which makes it, often, so dreary. We cannot accept the conventional view, built into the hierarchy of school knowledge, that the highest kinds of understanding are those that stand removed from personal concerns, human settings, and social relationships. In Kelly's terms, all learning is necessarily a personal affair. Yet its personal character is not reducible to the individualistic and pathological concepts which all too often become attached to certain children. On the contrary, the vision of learning as the extending of personal engagements in life makes no fundamental distinction in kind between pupils with 'special' or with 'ordinary' educational needs.

5 The process of learning

What happens when we learn something? The simplest idea of learning makes it a matter of adding bricks to the pile, accumulating more and more bits of information in our personal storehouse of knowledge. It was Piaget, above all, who showed how inadequately this idea describes the growth of understanding (see, for example, Piaget 1958). As his work vividly documents, intellectual progression does not entail knowing *more*, rather it is a matter of knowing *differently*. We do no justice to the thinking of 6-year-olds if we say only that they cannot grasp the principles of conservation. We have to acknowledge that, in their approach to number, substance, or volume, things add up in other ways, make their own, different kind of sense. Because he listened so carefully, so sensitively, to the children he questioned, Piaget was able to delineate the subjective worlds that precede conventional adult thinking, and to show them as a series of perfectly coherent approaches to life, each with its own distinctive logic. Piaget's contribution revolutionized our way of viewing intellectual growth. Learning could no longer be seen as the reception of ready-made understanding by empty vessels. Learners, however young, had to be respected as already possessing their own ways of understanding, making their own kind of sense of the curriculum at issue.

In Piagetian terms, learning has to be seen as an essentially qualitative process. Understanding does not proceed quantitatively, by a series of additive steps, but by significant changes of position, of angle of approach, changes in the whole perspective from which things are viewed. It is, as Kelly saw it, a matter of imaginative reconstruction. And just as, in concrete operations, children come to understand that the number of pieces of plasticine remains constant regardless of deformation processes which change their appearance, so older learners radically reconstruct the meaning of whatever they are engaged with, they approach it from an altogether different direction.

What this may mean is illustrated by an American study of practising teachers, carried out over twenty-five years ago by Runkel and Damrin (1961). Their subjects were secondary school teachers with different levels of professional training. In order to assess the effects of training on actual thinking about classroom situations, these investigators used a technique similar to that of the repertory grid (see Chapter 2, note 2). The teachers were invited to make judgements about twelve imaginary problem situations in school. Those judgements entailed selecting and ranking, from six possible kinds of information, the three which might be most helpful to a teacher for each problem in turn.

The problems included: an academically undecided student, a student who continually day-dreamed, an excessively rude student, a student who seemed chronically tired, and so on. The six kinds of information available were: school achievement, family and home life, intelligence, worries and fears, interests and ambition, and personality. Each teacher was free to make similar or different responses to each problem. The task involved may be clearer as represented by Table 1, showing an imaginary response.

Table 1 *Judgements, rank ordered from 1 to 3, of sources of information relevant to imaginary pupil problems*

	Ac. undecided	Day-dreaming	Rude	Tired	. . . 12
Achievement	3				
Family life			1	1	
Intelligence	2				
Worries		3	3	2	
Interests	1	2		3	
Personality		1	2		

This format allows the assessment of how teachers view a sample of potential problems, and, in particular, whether they are operating from a relatively simple or a relatively complex view. In the imaginary example above, where the four problems shown have each been treated differently, the pattern is quite complex. Obviously, a teacher who had made an identical pattern of response to two or more problems would be taking a rather simple view. It is possible, from this format, to locate the judgement of particular teachers somewhere within a whole range, from extreme complexity to extreme simplicity. It was on such structural aspects of teachers' perceptions that this study centred.

The central question with which Runkel and Damrin were concerned was with the effect, on the relative complexity of teachers' perceptions, of different levels of training. So they compared three groups of teachers, with elementary, intermediate and advanced professional training levels. The relation between level of training and complexity of perception, as it emerged, was not linear, but curvilinear. The pattern that emerged is shown below.

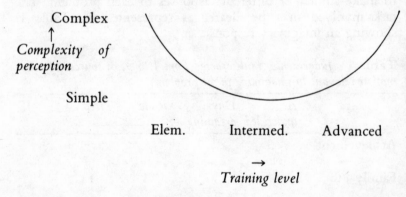

Teachers whose training has been minimal, on this evidence, operate quite a complex view of potential problems in school. Gaining further training, it seems, leads to a much simpler way of seeing things. But still further training entails adopting a perspective just as complex as before.

These findings seem to challenge many of the ways in which we usually think about learning. Certainly they cannot be fitted into an additive model. If the development of understanding, through prolonged educational experience, entailed quantitative growth, then the graph of change would just go on going up as level of training increased. But even given a qualitative definition of learning, it is hard, at first sight, to make sense of the kind of progression which emerged in Runkel and Damrin's study. How could teachers undergoing further professional training come to adopt a simpler view than the one taken by teachers whose training had been less advanced? This is very difficult to square with our usual assumption that learning involves realizing that things are *more*, not *less*, complicated than we had previously imagined.

In order to understand this apparently paradoxical change, we need to look to the ways in which people test out what they have learned. Again, it was Piaget who demonstrated the constant reference to the external world that any learner must make. In learning something, we necessarily re-work the balance between assimilation and accommodation. For this, to experience the non-viability of our existing understanding is crucial. We find, to our surprise, our dismay, that we cannot really grasp why things turn out as they do, cannot anticipate what will happen next, cannot get a leverage on what is essentially involved in the area we are struggling with. It is, most fundamentally, the *unsuccessful* outcome produced by putting our existing understanding to the test which represents an essential experience in our learning endeavour. In Kellyan terminology, the key to reconstruction is invalidation[1] – that is, the disconfirmation of what we had expected.

The study of Runkel and Damrin suggests that learning proceeds in qualitatively different steps. The teachers who had reached the stage of advanced professional training had presumably themselves passed through the kinds of thinking associated with earlier stages. They had begun, following initial training, by seeing school problems, and their resolution, as no simple matter. If during further training, they reduced their learning of schooling and its problems to a crudely simplistic level, it was because only then could they clearly test it out. If they subsequently proceeded to build a more complicated view for themselves, this was because the validational outcomes of their simplified understanding had shown it to be inadequate, to require further elaboration. It was then possible for them to build, since some foundation existed.

As a first-year student of psychology, I strove, with little success, to make personal sense of the courses I was doing. The central nervous system, psychopathology, statistics, psychometrics, moral philosophy, theories of development – I could not make it all add up. Then, at a conference of the British Psychological Society, I heard a psychopharmacologist describe the work she was doing, analysing brain chemistry: 'Serotonin', she pronounced, 'keeps the brain sane'. Immediately, the whole of psychology fell into place for me. It was a complete revelation. I saw, with exhilarating clarity, how everything reduced to this one profound principle. Returning to my family for the vacation, I felt able at last to answer their questions with total conviction. Why did two children in the same family develop so differently? 'Oh, just different levels of serotonin.' How could psychology explain humour? 'Only a matter of variation in the areas of serotonin secretion.' What accounted for juvenile delinquency? 'Well, the brains of some young people failed to produce the right amount of serotonin.'

This happy situation could not, of course, last for long; inevitably, I soon became all too clearly aware of the limits of my simple explanations. As I went on living with the idea that every psychological question could be answered by reference to serotonin, it gradually came to seem more and more inadequate. As I remember it, this happened in a number of different ways. Partly, it was that this kind of explanation sat very uneasily with some of my other longstanding convictions. If I really held to it, I should have to give up ideas that had for many years seemed deeply true – ideas about the importance of how people felt about their situations, their lives. Then, as I heard and read, in my official studies, what psychologists had 'found out' about human functioning, there was little evidence that could honestly be fitted into explanations in terms of brain chemistry. I also talked to friends and fellow students, and particularly to another woman studying psychology, with whom I regularly shared interests, problems, excitements. Encountering her kindly scepticism, and that of others, about my great discovery acted to put a serious question mark over its viability. Yet, it was from this point that I began to develop the rudimentary beginnings of my personal ideas in psychology. Paradoxically, what I eventually came to believe had no room in it for psychopharmacology. Yet the 'serotonin experience' had, I believe, been crucial in allowing me to evolve my own kind of psychology. Through this experience, I had begun a real personal engagement with the area, and because of this I had created possibilities for myself of making sense of it all.

If we look at learning in this way, it seems clear that the process is not one of steady incremental progression. It takes a far more wayward course, often descending into total confusion, and lurching into grossly oversimplified formulations. And what is critical, apparently, for movement forward is that our present ways of understanding things can be put to the test, opened up to validational outcomes. Only if what we think we know can somehow be challenged, and events made to yield evidence as to its validity, its fertility, is it possible to take things further – to learn. Yet useful validation and invalidation – to use Kelly's terms – do not seem, on reflection, to be a simple matter.

There is, of course, quite a large literature about the place of validational outcomes in human learning. Perhaps one of the most influential lines of thought has been a broadly behaviourist one, which gives central importance to the concept of feedback. Since the fundamental assumption of this approach is that people learn through reinforcement, careful attention is paid to ensuring that every learner response is met with quick and appropriate feedback. In this rationale, it is a matter of concern that, in classroom learning, *what* is wrong is often quite unclear. A boy gets back his maths homework, duly corrected; some answers are ticked, others crossed. He can really have no certainty, for the erroneous solutions, just where he made the wrong decisions, took the incorrect path. Even if the teacher takes him through each sum, showing the calculations he should have made, he will not necessarily come to understand exactly how he went astray. More precise, individually tailored feedback is needed, so that at each step of the way, he is positively or negatively reinforced, and so learns, as he goes along, what is the correct response at each stage. That way, he will check his errors first time around, instead of repeating them, learning wrong rather than right reactions, and thereby making them habitual.

Another branch of the same logic makes crucial the avoidance of incorrect responses, by forestalling the possibility of pupils making mistakes. Through the worksheet series, the computer-assisted instructional programme, learners are carefully steered towards right answers, correct solutions. From one viewpoint, this situation is benign. No one endures failure; every pupil experiences success. Yet, as most teachers would probably see it, this approach does little justice to the development of understanding, as against merely mechanical kinds of learning. It is, perhaps, rather a matter of good performance – jumping through the hoops of the circus ring under the direction of a skilled and kindly ring-master.

In a behaviourist approach, the significance for learning of validational evidence is reduced to a simple matter of being told that you are right or wrong. If right, you can repeat the same response next time; if wrong, you must change it. Yet a clear awareness of being wrong is no guarantee of further learning. As many pupils – and many teachers – find, it is quite possible, in classroom contexts, consciously to repeat the same mistakes over and over again. Despite the familiarity of the situation, the clear recognition of how badly you did things previously, the horrible anticipation that this may happen again now, there seems no way of breaking out of the vicious circle. Yet again, the third-year pupil exposes her non-comprehension in the geography lesson. The teacher, for the umpteenth time, rises to the teacher-baiting of his class.

If conscious mistakes do not, of themselves, act to facilitate new learning endeavours, this is because no alternative ways of understanding seem to be available. We go wrong again because we have no choice. It is only when we can glimpse other possibilities, sense that there might be other, personally meaningful ways of doing things, that finding ourselves wrong may be enabling rather than disabling. In some sense, learners need validational evidence which is both negative and positive – confirming and disconfirming at the same time.

A first-year secondary pupil invited, in his humanities class, to try his hand at composing a report for an imaginary tabloid, feels totally at a loss. Nothing he has done up till now, in his school work, seems to have prepared him for this task. All he can do is produce the kind of standard school essay which has previously served in English lessons. But this is not what his teacher is after. She will, perhaps, only succeed in conveying a message of personal inadequacy: the boy feels confirmed in his suspicions that, after all, humanities is not for him. Or perhaps his teacher can speak to something rather different in this pupil – his lively sense of the modes through which TV presenters characteristically address their audiences. Suddenly the task assumes another character for the boy; he begins to envisage how he might engage with it in an entirely new way. Whereas, previously, written work was all much-of-a-muchness, it now seems to entail various different possibilities. There are alternatives available and choices to be made. The next time this boy finds he has 'gone wrong' in his writing, the experience may be rather different, because he now has personal access to other avenues which might be explored.

In the traditional model of education, which assumes the transmission of ready-made understanding, validational outcomes are implicitly defined in terms of right and wrong. If knowledge is absolute, pupils either possess it or they do not. In a constructivist model, validation has quite a different character. Knowledge, in whatever sphere, is never final. What essentially matters is its *viability* in practical, personal and social terms. No one formulation has sole rights. There are always many possible ways of defining things. Helpful validation then becomes, not a matter of final arbitration, but of simultaneously affirming and challenging existing constructions of meaning.

It is on questions such as these that the work of Douglas Barnes (1986) has been particularly illuminating. In his argument, school learning essentially consists in making connections between the 'action knowledge' of day-to-day experience and the specialized knowledge offered within the school curriculum. Children can eventually make sense, for instance, of the specialized terminology of physics only if they can first enter the area within the terms of their everyday experience. Because of the multiple daily pressures they face, many teachers cut short the opportunities for this vital early engagement, concentrating instead on the need for pupils to master the technical vocabulary of the subject. Yet it is only when children are offered space and encouragement for trying out their own, 'lay' formulations on the topic, that they can make a personal entry into it. Here is one physics teacher who, as Barnes argues, succeeds in facilitating this process.

T *This is almost the same as that one . . . a slightly different arrangement . . . cut in half . . . you see it? . . . little tin can . . . silver thing in the middle . . . silver thing with circles on it? . . . that's that tin can . . . tin can just like that one . . . all right . . . on a good day then what is going to happen to the shape of that? Is it going to go . . . down? . . . Do you know? . . . See what happens to the pointer. Well that pointer is going to be connected. . . .*

It seems reasonable to assume that this teacher's unusual language, informal and yet exactly adjusted to the apparatus, is related to his pupils' equally unusual degree of active participation in the lesson. This cannot have been merely the result of the teacher's linguistic style, but of what his speech itself implied, an interest in and attentiveness to the pupils' understandings and their attempts to extend them. Because he attended to their struggle to understand as well as to his goals as a teacher of physics, he was able to set up in his lessons an exchange of interpretations based on demonstrations with apparatus which boys and girls of quite limited ability were able to join in, and which even encouraged them to ask questions of their own. Such exchanges were sadly infrequent in the other lessons on which this paper was based, but it would be misleading to attribute this to the teacher's informal style alone. What we saw in this lesson was a teacher who presented apparatus which symbolized visually the principles he wanted his pupils to grasp, and who listened attentively to their attempts to think aloud about it. He showed that he took their contributions seriously, validating their efforts to understand by replying to them rather than evaluating them, as teachers frequently do in an attempt to control relevance. It seemed that it was his success in validating his pupils' thinking that made their participation in his lessons different from others, and encouraged them to initiate new issues and explore them aloud. Since it would be nearly five years before any of these pupils would have to demonstrate in an examination their ability to write formal scientific prose, he was surely right in placing his emphasis upon involving them in his thinking. Once a dialogue has been set up, the technical terms can be introduced in contexts which help the learners gradually to approximate their meanings to the teacher's, and eventually to adopt a style suited to writing about physics (Barnes, Britton and Torbe 1986, pp. 68–9).

In this interaction between a teacher and his pupils there is, as Barnes points out, a sense of warmth, of personal relationship. Without this it is difficult to see how children's 'action knowledge' could be elicited in classroom learning. In drawing upon their personal, out-of-school experience, trying out what it might mean in relation to the curriculum of lessons, pupils are necessarily offering something of themselves, their lives. This can only be done where the audience is personally known and trusted. Communication of ordinary experience, as against formal, technical propositions, does, anyway, presuppose sufficient mutual understanding for contributions to be met half-way – to be grasped intuitively through a familiarity with the personal world in which they are grounded.

It is precisely these qualities of personal relationship which make small friendship groups such a potentially effective context for the development of understanding. When friends talk together, they do so with genuine interest, support, encouragement and trust. If such talk is harnessed to the exploration of a lesson-related topic, it produces something very different from traditional classroom discourse. In his writings, Barnes provides many examples of the fertility of this small group talk. Fundamentally, when pupils discuss things with their friends, they talk for themselves and each other, rather than rehearsing second-hand statements in the interests of giving right answers. The equality of the relationship makes for freedom in expressing diverging viewpoints. Because no one's position is exclusively authoritative, there is no need to judge others invalid, or to foreclose issues in the interests of a hasty consensus. But the acknowledgement of difference carries with it a need to explain personal viewpoints, to formulate ideas and experience in ways that others can understand. This makes for a kind of responsibility for one's own learning which cannot exist where children feel they must submit themselves to another person's thought.

The transcripts with which Barnes illustrates this kind of talk characteristically involve quite rambling, even apparently inconsequential conversation. There is generally no very clear sequence. No explicitly defined 'problem' is pursued, nor is there seemingly a clear 'solution' of anything. Many thoughts seem only half-expressed. Some contributions get followed through, others not. Essentially, the children are talking in *provisional, exploratory* ways. They speak tentatively, try out their ideas on each other. There is clearly no need to defend opinions, or pretend certainties that are not felt. The mode is one of 'perhaps'.

By their own personal relationships with children, or by harnessing the children's own friendships, teachers can, on this evidence, sometimes create contexts in which pupils engage personally with the curriculum of lessons. Clearly, this cannot happen in a classroom atmosphere which is remote and impersonal. Children need intuitive understanding, and a sense of being valued, if they are to trust others with their personal experience. The context must be personally affirming, encouraging, if one is to speak tentatively, voice uncertainty, try out rudimentary ideas, and let others witness one's own faltering, groping, floundering early attempts at understanding. No one can risk being shown up as ignorant or silly in front of a critical audience. The essential, exploratory stage of learning is a delicate plant, needing space and protection.

What does all this imply for the place of validational outcomes in the development of understanding? If we see learning as neither incremental progression, nor a single unified process, the picture looks quite complicated. To engage themselves in an unfamiliar curriculum, children need initially to be allowed a period of 'milling around' in which they can try out, in tentative and provisional ways, what is the bearing on the topic, if any, of dimensions in personal experience. This stage is one of considerable vulnerability because it involves both personal exposure and confusion. If you are engaged in it you need a kind of validation of your quest, an encouragement to stay with it. 'Positive' or 'negative' feedback could hardly be less helpful. Being labelled either right or wrong forecloses thinking prematurely. You need, instead, a kind of suspension of evaluation, of arbitration, a suspension which allows the task to remain open.

The next stage of real learning is, perhaps, no less vulnerable. In the struggles of early exploratory thinking, those involved are likely to feel at a loss, often frustrated, even defeated. But out of this may come an exhilarating, yet essentially illusory, belief in total mastery. As the trainee teachers in Runkel and Damrin's study must have found, this phase seems in retrospect absurdly simplistic. I know that, had I risked my revelation about serotonin to an expert and critical member of academic staff, any confidence I had in my own thinking would have shrivelled up in shame and humiliation. Experience will, inevitably, throw doubts upon simple solutions, and prompt further efforts at revision. But again, the essential value of such early formulations needs to be affirmed. If these apparent insights are simply dismissed as incorrect, they cannot act as points of purchase on the area, hypotheses for which evidence can be sought, on which more elaborate formulations can be built.

On this argument, validation, in the form of personal support, personal encouragement, seems to play a vital role in learning. Yet this validation is clearly a long way from labelling answers right. Rather it is a matter of endorsing the viability, for the present, of the formulations offered by the learner. This does not carry the implication that such formulations are final, that there is no need fo; further exploration and possible recon-struction. On the same logic, invalidation, if it is to take learning further, must be something very different from the rejection of the learner's position as simply wrong. And it is here, perhaps, that a constructivist approach to knowledge offers an alternative.

Whereas the traditional transmission model can only insist on a single formulation of understanding, within a construc-tivist view many viewpoints are possible. This is surely the case, at least in principle, not just with the humanities, but with the more linear school subjects too. The present radical reconstruction of the maths curriculum demonstrates that there are multiple ways of structuring even this traditionally hard and fast area of learning. This does not, of course, deny that teachers' formulations of the curriculum carry greater auth-ority, more weight, and richer implications than those of pupils grappling with the subject for the first time. But it allows for the possibility that different ways of defining the area may be appropriate and acceptable at particular stages, and that, ultimately, children need to construct their understanding of the curriculum out of their own real experience. Given this, invalidation takes on a particular character. It is not a question of labelling answers wrong. It represents, instead, the offering of another viewpoint as a more elaborated, though not exclusive, way of seeing things. The close focus studies of Barnes vividly illustrate how, in the context of small group talk, it is the confrontation of different views of the world which acts as the impetus for developing understanding. But this can happen only within the framework which Kelly called constructive alternativism. Genuine learning happens, in the Barnes studies, in contexts of personal friendship where different perspectives are granted a kind of equality, rather than being judged against a standard of absolute truth. Many teachers also offer their pupils personal acknowledgement, liking, respect. Within such a relational context, children's early struggles with a new area of the curriculum are likely to meet with encouragement. And it is against this background of affirmation that more advanced views of the area, when suggested by teachers, can be seized on, because they represent exciting and intriguing alternatives, alternatives worth exploring.

6   The substrate of schooling

The learning process is a delicate plant; children, if they are to engage with the activities that schooling offers, need a climate that is individually attentive, individually affirming. The classroom context has, somehow, to encompass something of the firsthand experience, the street wisdom, that pupils bring, as particular and active agents in their own homes and neighbourhoods, with their own projects, feelings and hopes. It is when teachers, through background experience or imaginative empathy, can enter into the life-engagements of the young learners in their class that real educational breakthroughs are likely to occur. Through their personal understanding, such teachers are able to tailor the content of learning to the interests and life-knowledge of particular children, and to address their pupils, not in generalized, impersonal and didactic terms, but in the friendly, invitational discourse of ordinary social relations.

All this presupposes a large degree of freedom over the content of the curriculum and the modes of schooling. But teachers do not, of course, stand in total control over what or how they teach. And within the present climate of retrenchment, the constraints and pressures operating on the schooling system pose particularly serious threats to just these kinds of developments. The low status of education generally, indexed by poor teacher salaries, rundown buildings and dwindling resources, makes it highly vulnerable to such pressures. The directions towards which education is currently being pushed are broadly elitist and authoritarian. On the one hand, there are strong movements to undermine the comprehensive principle by setting up increasingly separate kinds of provision in schools. These implicitly reaffirm earlier values, in which only the traditional academic curriculum really counted. On the other hand – through the establishment, for instance, of government funded colleges, or of MSC courses in school – various manoeuvres are in operation to bring education under centralized control. One aspect of this is the attempt to impose a national curriculum.

This situation intrinsically threatens the kind of generous enlargement of school learning which is needed if education is ever to become genuinely personal. So far from allowing teachers to integrate school knowledge with children's own life experience, a return to traditional academic values entails a narrowing of the curriculum and the modes of teaching. Centralized control of content necessarily means a heavily normative approach. The situation and experience of minority groups of all kinds is likely to be excluded rather than affirmed within the learning context. Developing curricular areas which question the status quo will become increasingly difficult, as those whose lessons are under fire as 'too political' have already discovered.

For teachers working at the cliff-face of all this, many of these pressures are focused on the debate about 'standards' and the demand that schools should return to 'basics'. Mike Torbe (1986), an English specialist, offers a thoughtful discussion of this much-used term in present educational currency:

By 'the basics' is normally meant on the one hand a set of conventions concerning the appearance of writing – spelling, handwriting and punctuation – and on the other hand the ability to read, to count and to perform arithmetical calculations, and to produce on demand clear, readable written language. These 'basics' are often perceived as 'tools': the feeling is that without them learning is impossible. Such a view is not supported by what we know about the way people learn. It *is* important, for social reasons if for no other, that children should be able to perform successfully in these ways, but not if they do so at the cost of more important abilities. Among these, as a very different set of 'basics', consider the ability to understand how learning operates; to be able to use various kinds of talk, appropriate to various public and private contexts; to grasp the importance of social context itself and its general influence upon language use; to write for different purposes and for different audiences, in various styles and forms; and to use complex reference systems. Even to define them like this still falls short of what it is we should covet for children. What ought to be at the centre of attention is *what children's language can achieve for them*: things like the ability to use talk to get to know people they want to know, and to get on with those people they *have* to know; to use reading as a source of virtual experience, a way of living; to use both talking and writing as a means of discovering what they feel and think and of sharing that with others (Barnes, Britton and Torbe 1986, p. 139).

How the school curriculum might, at least in principle, be made into something like this is the focus of concern for Kieran Egan (1986). Like Torbe, Egan believes that reading, writing and counting – the 'basics' – are essentially irrelevant in themselves. Lying easily within the natural skills of children, their real significance consists in the worthwhile human uses to which they can be put. In Egan's philosophy, literacy and numeracy skills, like everything else in the orthodox curriculum, need to be approached from a particular broad direction. It is the part that each content area plays in the fundamental human story that provides its vital meaning. This story is the story of

A life and death struggle against ignorance, fear, poverty and hatred; it is a struggle for security, love, confidence and knowledge. And at its heart, whether one is athiest or religious, it is infused with mystery – most basically, the mystery of why there is existence rather than non-existence (Egan 1986, p. 121).

Such an approach puts a question mark over the conventional packages of school knowledge, which cannot come to life because they contribute nothing to children's understanding of their place in the human story. Science, for instance, is conventionally taught without reference to the human context in which it was constructed, or the human questions to which it has been addressed. It is, Egan suggests, as if scientific discovery had an existence and momentum of its own – as if it were 'a relentless, inhuman juggernaut'. Yet the real history and meaning of science is wayward, frightening, exciting. Scientific knowledge is inextricable from the curiosity, courage, frustration, persistence, of scientists; science cannot be separated from the real human world, in which teachers and children have their lives.

In Egan's account, the progression of schooling needs to be tailored to the sequence of stages through which children naturally pass – a sequence involving four successive kinds of access to the human world. Changes in *content* are not needed: like Jerome Bruner, Egan believes that any subject can be taught, honestly and effectively, at any age. Rather it is a matter of altering the form, the direction from which the subject is approached. If children are to engage with the curriculum, it has to be presented in terms currently available to them, in forms that they already use, eagerly and vitally, in their lives. These forms, so Egan believes, relate to four ways of experiencing the world: mythic, romantic, philosophic and ironic.

At the mythic stage, young children's access to knowledge is governed by the power of stories. What is comprehended is the dramatic interplay between the opposing, elemental forces of a larger than life world. This world is one of moral and emotional absolutes; it has few gradations, complexities or ambiguities. If the curriculum can be presented to young children in these terms, they can grasp it. When the material of early schooling is offered in dynamic, dramatic story form – forms in which conflict and tension develop before being finally resolved – young pupils will find their learning meaningful and involving.

In Egan's chronology, this stage is succeeded, at about 7 years, by the romantic stage, which lasts until about 14. Now, it is a vivid sense of separate identity, of individuals alone in a strange and threatening world, that informs children's perceptions. Power and the transcendence of limits are the preoccupations of this stage. This gives children an intense interest both in the context of reality and in the mental and physical feats of human beings within that context. There is a fascination with inventors, artists, explorers, scientists, heroes – 'the great' of every kind – a fascination to be engaged by a curriculum which locates knowledge in the lives of those who daringly constructed it. But the size and scope of the real world are also fascinating to children at this stage. The exotic, the fantastic, the spectacular, if they can be made to colour the content of school learning, evoke a sense of wonder and intellectual excitement. By contrast, a curriculum which seeks 'relevance' by dwelling only on what is local, everyday, familiar may simply evoke boredom. If school knowledge can be harnessed to themes of power and transcendence, children will sometimes call on impressive resources of effort and persistence. This is the stage at which young people often show a passion for detail, amassing huge mountains of facts, acquiring an encyclopaedic knowledge of some sphere that they have made their own.

If, at the romantic stage, the major theme is the possibility of overcoming ordinary limits, young people at the philosophic stage look at the world from a more complex viewpoint. This is a period, according to Egan, lasting from the mid-teens to around 19 or 20. Here, the essential concern is with establishing the place of human life within the whole natural, social or philosophical order. Where the romantic phase entails a dwelling on facts for their own sake, a collection of particular or out-of-way knowledge about the world, young people at this later stage are interested in broad maps which define reality in terms of comprehensive laws or principles. Ideology is now dominant. This concern demands a school curriculum which presents knowledge in relation to abstract concepts and theoretical frameworks – as material that may serve as evidence, or as challenges to particular ideologies. It is this preoccupation with ultimate meaning, with constructing a total world view, which, Egan suggests, often makes for such an eager engagement at this stage with psychoanalytic or Marxist theories, or with abstract concepts such as quarks and black holes.

In Egan's argument, the adequacy of thinking at the philosophical stage depends on how far the romantic stage has been nourished. Only if, in the preceding period, children's natural absorption in the real world has been encouraged and fostered, can the grand schemes of the next period be more than merely shallow and facile. And similarly, the philosophic stage acts to prepare the ground for the final, ironic stage. At about 20, some young adults begin to develop another kind of outlook, in which one single ideology ceases to govern their thinking. There is a recognition that particulars alter cases, that every theory, however useful, has its limits. This altered way of seeing things does not, however, come about automatically. It is a product of the thinking which young people have already done, particularly with teachers who have themselves moved into the ironic stage. Such teachers are able, while encouraging philosophical inquiry, to help young people not merely to gather knowledge which supports an ideology, but to become aware of anomalies, and, ultimately, to adopt a more open and questioning position towards final truths.

Egan's developmental scheme, with its implications for the curriculum, is unusual and intriguing. His ideas do, however, seem somewhat idealistic. For instance, a history of science needs to take account of certain rather ugly facts. As Robert Young has shown, scientific research in medicine has been systematically applied to the development of marketable products, at the expense of simple public health measures to eliminate disease in the third world. Actually to implement any new conceptual model, such as Egan's, would entail a comprehensive reorganization of the modes and content of schooling. Egan's categories cut across the conventional divisions of primary, secondary and tertiary. More fundamentally, the whole examination system, with its hold on what may be offered in secondary classrooms, would need to be drastically revised. There are hopes, currently, that GCSE may represent a new orientation towards assessment; but given present exigencies, really radical changes seem unlikely. It is no accident that where teachers have, in practice, created a more personal curriculum, this has been in spheres of schooling that lie outside formal certification – in pastoral and active tutorial work, in health education and, increasingly, in the growing area of personal–social education (PSE).

Personal–social education is rooted, most broadly, in the recognition that mainstream schooling offers young people an inadequate preparation for the lives that most of them will lead. In conditions of mass unemployment, the traditional curriculum appears grossly irrelevant. Its content is clearly remote from the experience, situation and problems that young people will actually face in their lives. The qualifications at which this curriculum is aimed are unattainable for the majority of school leavers. In the argument of the influential Hargreaves Report,[1] the curriculum needs to be greatly broadened, to include personal and social education, if it is to meet the real needs of young people living in our society.

Against this background it is, of course, the future situation of secondary school pupils which has loomed large in the way PSE has been developed. If most young people face, at best, prospects of short-term, semi-skilled employment interspersed with periods of unemployment, what do they need from schooling? Many people have been concerned to improve individual stakes in the sparse job market. Perhaps at least school leavers can be helped to construct their own Record of Personal Achievement to impress employers, or learn to deal efficiently with the processes of job application. Another concern has been to prepare young people for 'leisure', by helping them develop resources for personal interests, or by fostering personal qualities which may serve to cushion them against the frustration and emptiness of unemployment.

PSE stands apart from the traditional school curriculum

because it is, typically, outside the sphere of formal examinations. And a central plank in its rationale has been the need to involve young people in the construction of their own learning. Given freedom from the relative constraints of examination boards, learners can be offered far greater responsibilities than is usually possible. Not only can they help to construct their own curriculum, within the broad terms of reference defining its goals, but it is also possible to open up the *assessment* of learning so that young people, individually or in groups, can actively negotiate with teachers the criteria by which learning should be evaluated, and the judgements, on these criteria, of their own achievements. PSE tutors have been among the pioneers of methods such as profiling and records of achievement – assessments in which young people themselves participate, which do not involve invidious comparisons, and which focus on what the young person *can*, rather than *cannot*, do.

In practice, the assessment of PSE has generally entailed one of two kinds of currency. The aims have been defined as either the development of personal qualities, or the acquisition of social and life skills. Personal qualities, like confidence, initiative, reliability or co-operation, will, it is assumed, stand young people in good stead in living generally, and more specifically in facilitating their negotiation of the job market. Yet, for all their apparent credibility, these educational aims are not without problems. Judging a young person to be confident means that behaviour in the classroom is generalized, and it is assumed that behaviour in every other situation will be similar. The initiative shown within an educational activity is taken as an index of initiative in life projects generally. This means that the classroom context is unquestioningly assumed to offer young people every possible opportunity for personal investment. However, as many teachers are all too well aware, this is very often far from true. The activities to which adolescents commit themselves most seriously, in which they feel most confident, show initiative, prove reliable, and co-operate most effectively, may exist in a very different sphere from that of the classroom.

Making personal qualities the focus of PSE also ignores the fact that the full and free expression of 'personality' is possible only within genuinely personal relationships. Classroom relationships, however good, are necessarily constrained by their institutional context, which entails basic inequalities of power. This makes the school setting an inappropriate one for the demonstration of qualities which can emerge only within intimate contexts, or those to which young people bring maximum personal commitment. And the demand that adolescent pupils reveal themselves, 'come out' personally in school is, perhaps, tantamout to riding rough-shod over the personal guardedness and reserve which many young people, understandably and legitimately, feel towards the institutions of schooling.

The assessment of personal qualities is, necessarily, a value-laden judgemental process. Those defined as desirable are, typically, part of a 'good citizen' complex. The norms which they implicitly carry are ultimately those of dominant social groupings. They endorse the value of being universally polite and forthcoming, of automatically deferring to those in authority, of conforming with the existing order. No rough edges are allowed. And if this is true of personal qualities, it applies still more seriously to the other goal of PSE – social skills and competences.

Those who utilize concepts of social skills generally talk in common-sense terms about the meaning of these concepts. Questions of value are sidestepped by the appeal to 'what actually works'. Training in self-presentation or communication skills does, for instance, apparently improve young people's chances in securing work. This seems at first sight quite unproblematic. But the approach inevitably depends on an uncritical acceptance of the official organization of labour – with its ageist and sexist practices, its vested interests, its exclusion of the black economy, and so on. More broadly, social or life competences cannot but incorporate an endorsement of the social status quo. If 'what works' is to be the measure of social skill, then young people will need training in strategies that conform to, rather than question, existing power relations in our society.

Essentially, both these approaches disregard the real personal and social position of young people. They pre-empt a positive orientation towards the establishment. Because this orientation is defined as 'skill', its real moral character escapes notice. Yet such a definition acts to reduce social intercourse to a battery of circus tricks, and divorces social action from the felt allegiance, respect, affection or solidarity which is its real basis.

The approach advocated in this book has, as its fundamental

concern, the personal reality of the individual learner. Unlike the concepts of personal qualities or social competences, this approach locates the definition of learning within the personal subjectivity of learners themselves. So, far from setting up, as arbiters, other people whose reactions, comparative judgements and values are entailed in deciding how confident or socially skilled a young person is, personal construct psychology defines learning as a matter of personal understanding. Only you yourself, as the learner, can know if you have understood something, and only you can say what that understanding means for you. Within the crucial area with which PSE is concerned, how should that understanding be defined? Surely it is psychological understanding, in its broadest sense, which is basically at issue.

As members of a society, each of us has to achieve a workable understanding of our social world. It is the psychology we construct which allows us to define ourselves in relation to others, which underlies our moment-to-moment dealings, our social transactions, and governs the stances we take up, the projects we launch in the course of our lives. Of all spheres of understanding, psychological understanding is arguably the most essential. Certainly, without it we are lost. That this is so, is clear from an unusual piece of research conducted some years ago by Don Bannister (1962–6).[2] Describing it will entail stepping aside, for a time, from issues directly concerned with schooling.

Among the many forms of personal breakdown which human beings can experience, thought-disordered schizophrenia is probably by far the most serious. For those who suffer this condition, the ordinary everyday world becomes gradually more and more incomprehensible. Strange visions may inexplicably appear and disappear. Alien voices may suddenly utter terrifying judgements, or make bizarre commands. The meaning of events becomes elusive, puzzling; nothing can be taken for granted. Intimate friends seem different and alien; even one's own behaviour appears mysterious. To suffer this kind of breakdown means, of course, becoming as strange to others as to oneself; of all psychiatric conditions, thought-disordered schizophrenia is the most enigmatic.

It was this condition which Don Bannister, inspired by personal construct psychology, set out to explore. He did so by examining the kinds of interpretations which thought-disordered schizophrenics seemed to place – however tentatively, however temporarily – on their social worlds. Did people in this condition make any sense at all of themselves in relation to others? Could they find meaning of any kind in the world of social action and interpersonal relationships? Using the repertory grid technique, the sorting task described earlier (see Chapter 1, note 1), Bannister invited a number of psychiatric patients suffering this condition to make judgements of photographed faces, guessing, as well as they could, what kinds of people they were – how mean, kind or sincere they were, for instance.

When someone undertakes this kind of provisional judgement, they necessarily draw on their own psychology. This typically means that, within the set of judgements they are asked to make, there are positive correlations between kindness and sincerity and negative correlations between kindness and meanness. Such correlations do, of course, reflect the obvious fact that, in our ordinary shared psychology, the meaning of kindness and sincerity partly overlaps, while that of mean is partly opposite to that of kind. For thought-disordered schizophrenics, however, no such relationships emerged; it was as though they had made all their judgements entirely randomly.

On the face of it, this situation is not very surprising. Thought-disordered schizophrenics seem both bewildering and bewildered; one would, perhaps, hardly expect that in a complex task such as this they could produce any very meaningful judgements. But the next step in Bannister's research showed that this condition is not one of generalized confusion; it specifically entails *psychological* understanding. By this stage, I had joined the research project. We now asked the same thought-disordered schizophrenics to make judgements about the physical characteristics of objects. They were invited to consider such items as a drawing pin, a loaf of bread, a washing machine, and so on. How large, heavy, easy to move about, were these objects? Again, we compared the judgements of thought-disordered schizophrenics with those of other people. There was little difference. Just like anybody else, these patients saw a negative relationship, for instance, between being heavy and being easy to move about. This condition does not, therefore, involve a loss of understanding about the world of physical space and physical entities. Rather, this most serious breakdown is a breakdown of the capacity to make sense of the whole social fabric – a loss of the ability to 'read' people and their interrelations. It is this failure which proves fatal to personal viability.

Given the huge complexity of the social world, it is, perhaps, hardly surprising that many people fail to develop a workable personal psychology, or that, in other cases, the psychology they have constructed proves unable to make sense of their experience. To all of us, surely, the behaviour of other people is often surprising, puzzling or disturbing. You do not need to enter a foreign country to feel yourself a stranger among others. For a girl just starting secondary school, the world she has entered is altogether alien. Nothing her older brother has told her has prepared her for the sheer unfamiliarity of this culture, with its unknown rules, expectations, dealings and characterizations. Nor is it only new people, new settings, which challenge our personal psychologies. Those whom we know most well, most intimately of all, many act to undermine our confident assumptions. By behaving in altogether unanticipated, unlooked-for ways, parents, children, lovers, spouses or friends can shatter – perhaps for a time, perhaps for ever – the very foundation of the understanding by which we live.

All this means that *psychology*, in its broadest sense, represents the most significant, the most fundamental, kind of understanding. Though, fortunately, few people develop the complete breakdown of their psychology which we know as schizophrenic thought disorder, we all at times have to struggle to understand some happenings in our personal–social worlds. And if viable psychological understanding is not easily maintained, neither is it quickly developed. As Dorothy Brierley (1967) first showed, children take time to construe their social worlds in truly psychological terms. Brierley asked children aged 5 to 16 years to make comparisons between people they knew. There was a clear developmental progression in the kinds of comparisons made. The youngest children talked in essentially concrete ways, using physicalistic descriptions: 'She gives me things', 'He's fat'. Or they might make very global evaluative judgements, such as 'They're nice'. A few years later, most children referred to less directly accessible aspects of people, or offered personal evaluations that were qualified, or substantiated. A 9-year-old might, for instance, describe someone as 'kind, because she listens to you'. Many constructions at this stage were in terms of skills or social roles: 'He is a good footballer', 'They're teachers'. Only in the early or mid-teens did genuinely psychological categorizations start to appear: 'They're both fun to be with because they're interested in lots of different things.' 'She is not very happy, and that's why she is so spiteful.' These terms, in making reference to subjective aspects of other people, are essentially inferential. To the extent that we can use them in understanding others and ourselves, they free us from the tyranny of the obvious, the immediate, from crude and physicalistic interpretations. They allow us to 'read' each other imaginatively, rather than just literally. Although, like any other sphere of construing, our social understandings cannot be final and may, perhaps, often need re-working, nevertheless a psychological kind of understanding offers the only real basis for viable social engagement.

What part does schooling play in the development of psychological understanding? On the face of it, it is only PSE or the pastoral areas of school which make children's psychology their central concern. Less focally, psychology features in certain spheres of the more formal curriculum: social studies, humanities or child development. Yet ultimately, the psychology of social relationships is deeply implicated as a substrate in *all* the dealings of school – in the whole complex network of transactions which we call the hidden curriculum. It is just because this curriculum does remain hidden, that opportunities for children to articulate, share and develop their own psychology typically go unused.

Part of the hidden curriculum covers the status of knowledge, knowing and knowers within the setting of schools. Traditionally, school knowledge has an absolute character, and comes to be possessed by pupils to whom teachers transmit it. Although many teachers would dissociate themselves from such a model, it still largely governs the whole pedagogy of school. One aspect of this is that learning is typically viewed as involving products rather than processes. Yet, whatever curriculum is at issue, its meaning is, necessarily, personally constructed and reconstructed by particular teachers and learners. And the process of construing is itself an essentially psychological one.

Some years ago, Estelle Philips (1982) worked with a design and technology teacher interested in opening up his curriculum.

In the first lesson of a first-year secondary class, Phillips invited the children to do an exercise. The class itself was mixed, and included some pupils who had previously done craft work in school, along with others who had not. Each child was asked to consider twelve manufactured objects: a saw, a bicycle, a 'Marmite' jar, a plastic toy duck, a brick, and so on. Phillips invited the children to think individually about these items in successive triads. Considering the saw, the bicycle, the 'Marmite' jar, which two would they put together, apart from the third? What was the similarity, and the difference? How about the 'Marmite' jar, the toy duck and the brick? The children worked their way through six triads, writing down the dimensions of similarity and difference for each in turn. Their judgements were then put up on the board, and the class group was invited to discuss what they saw.

To the pupils in this group, this material proved unexpected and fascinating. Not everyone, it was evident, made the same kind of sense of this realm of common experience. For a boy to whom the saw and bicycle were obviously alike because they were made of metal, as against the glass of the 'Marmite' jar, his classmate's comparison in terms of opaqueness and transparency came as a surprise. Dimensions of meaning also emerged as unexpectedly different in involving dissimilar contrasts. To one child, ornamental might be contrasted with ugly; to another, with useful. As well as differences in perception, commonalities also became apparent. Some of these related to gender; there were certain dimensions of comparison which only boys used, others that were produced only by girls. And, it was clear, a previous experience of craft lessons created some common ground. Those with experience of such lessons tended to use rather similar categorizations, where those without tended to be more idiosyncratic.

On one level, all this is unsurprising. Given the nature of the task, one might anticipate that children's construing of a set of manufactured objects would be partly similar, partly dissimilar, and that both gender and previous experience with the curriculum might influence their perceptions. Yet making this material explicit – making it the focus of discussion and reflection – acted to articulate the essentially implicit basis of learning. The exercise allowed both the children and their teacher to acknowledge that there are very many possible ways of looking at the world of manufactured objects, that being a girl rather than a boy entails a rather different perception of this world, and that the school curriculum entails its own specialized perceptions – some perceptions sitting closely with the constructions already available to children, while others are more remote. This way of engaging pupils with school learning makes explicit the constructive nature of knowledge. It recognizes all children as already making their own kind of sense of the curriculum. But beyond that, this kind of exercise locates school learning within the personal psychology of learners. Philips's study demonstrated to pupils themselves something of the relation between school knowledge and their existing understanding. It also showed how far, within the context of an ostensibly neutral task, the ramifications of gender involve partly differentiated kinds of perceptions.

Gender was the central focus of the work of another secondary school teacher, Rachel Miller. In the study already mentioned (Salmon and Claire 1984), I studied something of the ways in which Miller used her drama lessons to develop the psychological understanding of her pupils. The second year, which Miller had just taken over, was, at first, divided on blatantly sexist lines. Girls and boys sat as far apart from each other as they could. There was little real communication across these battle lines, only a regular hostile and derisive commentary from the boys, met by a sullenly resentful, defensive reaction on the part of the girls. It was to this situation that the teacher's drama work was essentially addressed.

Miller used every opportunity in her lessons to facilitate the mutual entry of boys and girls into the situation and experience of each other. Sometimes, particular pupils were invited to improvise a role in which they took the part of the other gender; not surprisingly, this happened more often with girls playing male roles than the other way round. This situation was one of considerable personal exposure and potential vulnerability. More frequently, this teacher asked the pupils to work in safer and less individualized ways. For instance, the children, working in supportive, same-sex friendship groups, would prepare a script which would eventually be spoken by children of the other gender. Before the script was finalized, however, it had to be negotiated with those who would speak it. This necessarily entailed much detailed cross-checking as to the likely feelings and reactions of those across the gender divide.

In order to accomplish tasks such as these, the girls and boys in Miller's class had of necessity to move beyond their mutual antagonism and stereotyping. No one can speak for another person, or prepare what that person should say, without trying to step into that person's own particular shoes. However inaccurately a boy may portray the girl or woman he is representing, the very effort to understand her situation, her experience, as it feels to her, must involve him in a radical change of stance. The female world is no longer merely the object of routine mockery, but a sphere that can be personally entered. To the extent to which they involve themselves in this, boys and girls can begin to hear each other, to learn something of the other's intentions, hopes and problems, to appreciate sympathetically what it is like to belong to the 'opposite' gender.

Miller also set up a complicated guessing game to help her pupils go beyond sexist perceptions. Again in the context of small, same-sex friendship groups, the children talked together for the first half of the lesson. Their task was twofold. Each group member was to tell their friends the story of some incident – exciting, frightening or funny – in which they had been personally involved. The group then decided which incident they wished to share with the whole class, and who among them was to tell it. The story was rehearsed for this public telling. In the second half of the lesson, the teller in each group in turn offered the story, speaking in the first person. The audience had to guess whose incident it really was. Had it happened to the pupil who told it, or to one of their friends, and if so, which one? In order to make such judgements, the children had to consider each other very carefully. They needed, if they were to move beyond random guesses, to appreciate, quite fully and delicately, the highly differentiated identities and experience of each group member. Merely stereotypic categorization by gender was an inadequate basis for such judgements. Again, this task obliged boys and girls to move out of global and hostile mutual perceptions, to begin to appreciate something of the real complexity and individuality of each others' personal positions.

In Kellyan terms, social relations are constructed out of mutual perceptions. To the extent that two people are committed to trying to understand each other's ways of seeing things – their individual viewpoint, their basic stance in life – they can maintain a genuinely social relationship. If, on the other hand, each constantly approaches the other through categorizations that make no reference to that person's subjectivity, they cannot enter into a relationship. Most broadly, it is our willingness and ability to view people *psychologically* that defines how far we can understand and appreciate them – and how, as human beings, we will treat them. Sexism, like racism or classism, does not extend a properly psychological frame of reference to people across the divide; instead, they are lumped together, as objects rather than persons. Rachel Miller's insistence that other pupils be seen in psychological rather than merely objectifying terms, revolutionized relations in her classroom. After a year of this work, as was clear from classroom observation, group dynamics were altogether different; the currency of abuse and mockery had been abandoned, and boy–girl relations were characteristically mutually attentive, and, on occasion, mutually appreciative. Nor was this just the outcome of progress into adolescence, as was clear from a comparison of this class with others in the same school.

By its nature, our society acts to limit the range of personal sympathy, the imaginative appreciation, that, as its members, we accord each other. Power and privilege are unequally held, certain groups are grossly oppressed, choices and quality of life are hugely differentiated. This situation, for all that it is structured institutionally, is ultimately sustained by the psychology we hold. If schools are not merely to reproduce all the inequality, the injustice of society, the context of schooling must become an arena in which that psychology is carefully and critically examined. As the Humanities Project of Laurence Stenhouse showed,[3] the educational curriculum can, potentially, be used to open up vital aspects of the psychology which underpins racism. Pupils, working with teachers who are supportive yet questioning, can begin to articulate and reflect upon deeply personal attitudes towards their own and other ethnic groupings. In the process, the psychology that sustains racist practices can be acknowledged, questioned, and, perhaps, reworked.

As they start their secondary schooling, pupils are, on Brierley's evidence, themselves beginning to construct their own kind of personal psychology. This is, therefore, a critical period. Without the opportunity for reflection that schools – at least in principle – can offer, children will only remain under the tyranny of their particular local situation. They cannot hope to develop a broader and more generous psychology, which accords humanity to every participant in their social worlds. The exploration and development of psychological meaning as 'preparation for life' may in the end stand young people in better stead than the cultivation of narrowly defined and essentially conservative personal qualities or social skills.

7 Classroom relationships

When I first meet a group of adult students whom I am going to teach, I often begin with an exercise. I invite them all to attend to their perceptions of me. What kind of person, on this very brief and preliminary acquaintance, do I seem to be? I ask them to write down, for their own eyes only, the qualities which, provisionally, they judge me to possess. In the next part of the exercise, the students call out, not what they have actually written, but the *kind* of quality to which they have referred – the category, the aspect of people, which is involved in the judgement. I write all these categories up on the board.

This exercise always surprises people. It is the last thing students expect to do in the first session of a course they are taking. Their anticipations reflect widespread assumptions about education: that the personalities of teachers, like those of students, lie outside the domain of learning. Unless there are actually *problems*, in personal adjustment or interpersonal relations – problems which may get in the way of education – no attention needs to be paid, so we think, to the particular characteristics of those involved. With respect to the development of intellectual understanding, surely we are concerned with generalized, impersonal, academic content, and this is hardly a matter of individual persons? Making 'personality' the focus seems, in the light of these assumptions, to be taking a rather unserious, even frivolous approach towards the business of education.

As we continue to work on this exercise, the significance of the personal in the context of learning becomes more and more apparent. The material of discussion, as I mentioned, is the set of categories in terms of which the students have made their individual judgements of me. In Kellyan language, they represent a sample of their constructs about people. These constructs typically involve a whole variety of features: age, social class, educational background, level of warmth, confidence or sensitivity, attitude towards the students, and so on.

And given that these constructions are made within a shared social situation in which these young people are to act as 'students' to my 'teacher', they necessarily carry expectations as to our likely work together. If particular students refer to my age, my gender, my social class, this means that such aspects of people are, for them, features which *signify* – which entail important implications. As a middle-aged, middle-class woman, my viewpoint on things is, perhaps, more or less predictable. I can be expected, in my teaching, to adopt particular positions, to hold particular values, to understand and appreciate certain issues rather than others. For other students, different aspects are salient, relating, perhaps, to qualities of voice, manner or physical stance – qualities which seem to offer subtle clues of personal distinctiveness. Again, the constructs produced carry connotations as to my probable future relations with the students themselves and with the modes and materials of our shared future educational endeavour.

To each student who takes part in this exercise, I represent a particular kind of teacher, who is not the same as the one her neighbour is experiencing. All students construct their own particular person, and it is to that person that they then relate. Provisional though the construction may be, it nevertheless represents the starting point of that student's engagement with me. How these young people construe me governs their initial stance towards me, channels how they read me, defines the kind of messages they receive from me. This does not mean that early impressions simply become crystallized. As we go on talking, students often remark that they are having to revise their initial impressions. But, even if their first judgements prove, in the light of further acquaintance, to need some modification, they still constitute the basic ground of our encounter as teacher and student. That encounter, as it develops, may turn out differently from expectation. Yet the evidence is still evidence about those early constructs, or about their development. To this extent, first impressions do seem to be very important.

This exercise is not the way that most teachers begin their encounters with a new classroom group. Yet, though the task may be an unusual one, its essential concern is surely very familiar. In any learning situation, learners habitually, routinely, necessarily construe the new teacher, just as the teacher habitually, routinely, necessarily, construes the new class. My exercise does no more than make explicit the *basic work*, the fundamental construing of those involved, which underpins all formal learning. Without this essential personal sense-making, teachers and learners simply could not proceed – could not begin to address each other in particular ways, could not know what to make of the other's contributions. And for all that the construing of junior school pupils is far less complex and sophisticated than that of older learners, even the youngest children must make their own kind of sense of the teachers they encounter.

Here is the new teacher; your previous teacher has left to have a baby. For you, a 6-year-old girl in the class, he is obviously, disturbingly different. The lady teacher was small and young and pretty, she wore nice clothes and spoke in a quiet voice. This new teacher is quite old, and very tall and big. He has a loud voice, especially when he laughs. Before, you were getting on very well with your reading, and your mother was pleased with the books you took home. But now, there isn't much reading or writing, because you are always doing things in a big group. Your previous teacher always used to come up to the children, but this one calls out to you in front of the whole class. Everyone hears what you say, and often the teacher makes a joke about it, and they all roar with laughter.

This same teacher, so intimidating to one small girl in his class, may of course be quite differently construed by the boy who sits nearby. For this child, the teacher's encouragement of group activity, his tolerance of high levels of movement and noise within the classroom, his constant jokes and laughter, may come as a welcome relief. The teacher's physical presence seems comfortable, reassuring, enlivening. School, previously a place of difficulty and boredom, is now good fun, something to look forward to.

In this imaginary classroom, it is not only the children who engage in this kind of construing. The teacher, in taking over this class group, must also make his own sense of the person-alities within it – including the little girl who seems so shy and ill at ease, who responds so little, so mistrustfully to his suggestions and his jokes. If things are not to crystallize for ever in the initial fixture of difficult relations, this teacher must find some way of meeting his pupil's constructions. Genuinely personal encounters, personal dialogue, can proceed only out of shared dimensions of meaning. Where teachers and learners make the same *kind* of sense of things, see things essentially in comparable *terms*, then it is possible for them to communicate, to achieve mutual understanding. In every classroom, there are probably some children with whom, for their teachers, this proves to be a problem.

Pupils' and teachers' perceptions, of themselves and of each other, were the focus of a detailed study by Mary Baur (1981). Her basic concern was with the degree to which, in junior school classrooms, particular children shared their teacher's frame of reference. Because she expected that this would relate to a generally positive or negative teacher evaluation, she compared children who were described by their teacher as well, or as poorly adjusted. The children, who were 7 or 8 years old, were invited to describe some of the relationships in their classroom: 'Tell me about you and Sandra. What goes on between you? What are you like together?' They were asked about themselves in relation to a number of other children in the classroom, and in relation to the teacher, as well as about other children together and with the teacher. The teacher was invited to make parallel judgements. This allowed a comparison between the kinds of constructs which teachers and the pupils in their class used to describe the relationships within the shared world of the classroom.

What emerged from this study was that there was a much greater overlap between the teacher's frame of reference and that of the 'well-adjusted' than that of the 'poorly adjusted' pupils. Those defined as 'poorly adjusted' made little reference to classroom work in describing classroom relationships except in terms of its difficulty or their own low status. For teachers and for 'well-adjusted' children, work had great significance, not just in teacher–pupil, but even in pupil–pupil relationships. The 'well-adjusted' spoke of work in mainly positive and self-confident terms, alluding, for instance, to copying, helping or collaborating between children. Where they evaluated themselves or others, this was often according to classroom criteria such as the teacher herself tended to use. 'Poorly adjusted' children, who offered few such evaluations, tended to express a lack of confidence in themselves. Any excitement and imagination in their descriptions was typically reserved for matters outside school – concerns that were unrelated to classroom business. There was a similar contrast in construing classroom constraints. Whereas the 'poorly adjusted' made few references to these, except to getting into trouble over them, the 'well-adjusted' tended to speak from an insider's perspective – evidently understanding the teacher's expectations, knowing 'how to avoid her disapproval, or how to be surreptitious in "messing about" if they want to stay together'.

As Baur remarks, the judgements primary school teachers make of their pupils go largely uncontested; being the single teacher gives an authority to perceptions which is lacking in the secondary, multiple teacher context. This study showed the impact of a change of teacher on one of the classes studied. Many of the children previously defined as 'poorly adjusted' responded – on classroom observation, and in terms of their construing – much more positively to a teacher who brought a different frame of reference. The degree of affirmation which this teacher was able to offer some formerly problematic pupils, seemed to bring about a much more positive sense of themselves and their behaviour – a sense apparently closely linked with the teacher's own modes of construing.

This does not, of course, imply that such a teacher was able to construe every other child within the class group in positive, affirmative terms. In all classrooms, there will inevitably be some individuals with whom relationships are, and may remain, difficult. In the terms used here, the distance, the mutually alien character, of the personal meaning-systems involved, makes communication problematic. What counts for the teacher is something one particular pupil cannot begin to grasp. And what this pupil enjoys, rates, knows about – all this, so far as the teacher is concerned, is unknown territory. Only if, for her part, the teacher can learn something of this child's unfamiliar frame of reference, begin to look at things from that particular and different vantage point, will it be possible for her to build bridges between that individual life-experience and the world of school. The terms, the meanings that some children bring permit them to recognize, and engage with the ways in which teachers interpret themselves in relation to their pupils. For other children, the constructs that shape the world of school are less accessible, more mysterious. It is the teacher–pupil relationship which constitutes the interface between the two sets of meanings.

Among the 8-year-olds in Baur's study, teacher–pupil

commonality in perception was reflected in teachers' judgements of good or poor adjustment. These judgements must themselves have acted to confirm and maintain the relative closeness or distance in commonality. At this stage of school life, mutual alienation between teachers' and children's perspectives seldom turns out to be disastrous, perhaps because there is a greater openness and flexibility within junior classrooms than is characteristic of secondary ones. Later on, things are much less easily manageable. Given the multiple demands and constraints within which secondary teachers operate, young people who persistently misunderstand or refuse the role of pupil may prove, eventually, impossible to contain.

I was involved, a few years ago, in an investigation of suspension procedures within one local educational authority. This study, which was conducted by the Commission for Racial Equality (1985), had as its focus the question whether pupils of West Indian origin were being suspended from school in essentially discriminatory ways. In the course of the investigation, it became clear that black suspendees had very different profiles to those of white suspendees. Whereas suspended white secondary school children were generally fifth-year pupils, suspended black children were typically a year or so younger. White suspendees were, as a rule, young people with multiple problems. Not only did they show difficulties in their school life – truancy, low attainment, problems with other pupils – they also, frequently, had problems outside school involving contact with the police or the social services. None of this was characteristic of the black pupils who suffered suspension. For these young people, there were typically no notifiable problems outside school. Nor, within the school environment, did they generally present difficulties, being as a rule regular attenders, who got on well with other pupils, and had average or good levels of attainment. The meaning of these differences between the two groups was pointed up by the difference in the behaviour which had led to suspension. In the case of white pupils, this covered a range of behavioural offences, including persistent truancy, vandalism and destruction of school property, stealing from other pupils, and generally disruptive and aggressive behaviour. For black pupils, there was typically a single type of behaviour: threatened or actual violence towards particular teachers.

The evidence of this study points to a situation where, some-

times, relations between teachers and their pupils can deterio-
rate so far as to be unmanageable in school. The difficulty
does, in this situation, clearly reside, not within a generally
problematic pupil adjustment, but very specifically within the
relations between particular adolescents and particular teachers.
So problematic are these relations that the flashpoint is reached
much earlier than with pupils who are far more 'difficult',
more 'poorly adjusted'. Most teachers do not, happily, find
themselves in situations such as these with the non-white
members of their classroom groups. On the other hand,
impossibly difficult relations can and do arise with white pupils.
If, in this study, such relations typified interactions with
adolescents of West Indian origin, this merely reflects a wider
social situation of which schools form only a part. Given the
structural inequalities between white and non-white groups in
our society, a close accord of perspective is hardly to be
expected. Lack of commonality is built into the contrasting
situations, experience, biographies and futures of most black
young people and their white teachers. And this lack of
commonality is not merely a matter of mutual incomprehen-
sions of each other's background, culture or lifestyle. Classroom relationships act to define, to constitute, the positions of
those involved. This means that for pupils, as for teachers,
what happens in their encounters represents evidence of their
own social positions – positions in which each necessarily has
a vital personal investment.

When teachers find their black pupils problematic, this is
typically, it seems, to do with a particular kind of threat. In a
recent study, Christopher Driver (1981) sat in on a number of
classrooms in inner-city secondary schools and talked with the
teachers and pupils concerned. For a few white teachers, he
noted, the black members of their class group remained anony-
mously lumped together for quite a long time, unlike the white
pupils whose names were learned much earlier, as their identities became distinct. These particular teachers, though not
differentiating much among the black adolescents in their class,
tended to experience them as generally threatening and
provocative. This was partly because of the use of patois among
these young people, which, being unfamiliar, was felt to
exclude the teacher. Body language was also perceived to be
threatening. If these pupils were reprimanded, they did not
meet the teacher's eye, but looked down, apparently inattentive

and unconcerned. In face-to-face interaction, they often came to stand very close to the teacher, who experienced this as conveying possibilities of physical violence. Given the need to retain classroom control, all this was felt to have the potential to undermine or openly challenge the teacher's essential authority. Yet, Driver suggests, this reading was a *mis*reading. Eyes down, for these young people, indicated acceptance of the rebuke; physical closeness was the norm between speakers.

On this evidence, white teachers may sometimes misinterpret the behaviour of young black people by taking it to confirm their expectations of antipathy on the part of such pupils. But this is surely only part of the explanation. It ignores the fact that, on their side, black adolescents are themselves actively engaged, in the world of the classroom, in constructing, establishing, living out their own position. For many such young people, *their* experience is of being under threat. In setting up white teachers over black pupils, the classroom does, of course, recapitulate and re-present the power relations that govern the wider society. The mainstream curriculum offers a version of reality which affirms the value of the dominant white culture, while bypassing that of the black community and culture. These insults to black pride are compounded by teachers who seek to exclude the linguistic currency of black groups, or fail to learn and acknowledge the differentiated identities of black class members. To their relations with such teachers, many black adolescents may indeed bring a challenge; their stance may well be that of genuine confrontation. In these situations, the hostility is not just imaginary; the threat on both sides is perfectly real. The opponents on either side are, of course, typically cardboard cut-outs, stereotypes, rather than flesh-and-blood individuals. It is the caricature of black youth that the teacher faces – provocative, violent, lawless. On his side, the West Indian adolescent directs his anger at the very prototype of white oppression – arrogant, patronizing, dismissive.

Classrooms are complex social arenas. Although, when we think of them, we may focus on teacher–pupil relationships as though they were independent entities, in fact they are inextricable from relations between pupils themselves. When a black adolescent boy confronts and challenges his teacher, he does so for an audience. His defiance carries with it the intimate understanding, the unspoken endorsement, of his mates in the class; what happens next has significance for them too. The move he has made implicates not just himself, but his peers, and it will have subtle ramifications for his social standing among his friends and associates.

Children perceive their teachers, engage with them, not in a vacuum, but within a whole surrounding network of social relationships. These relationships, because they are vital to young people, have to be taken into account in how they as individuals relate to particular teachers. Those who teach come to be constructed in distinctive ways by groups of children, who make reference to these constructions in their individual interactions with the teachers concerned. To ignore or challenge the position of your own reference group, as a pupil, is to find yourself out on a limb, as I personally discovered in my changed relation with my Latin teacher. Sometimes, of course, a teacher can become redefined by the group through subtle kinds of social reorientation. Once feared and disliked, a woman history teacher is now known as strict but fair, someone to be respected. The nature of engagement with this teacher has been significantly altered. The consensus within children's social groupings directs and constrains the teacher–pupil relations of individuals, and carries its own interpretation of their particular encounters.

Social relationships among themselves are, for most young people, by far the most important part of their school lives. Sometimes, alas, they represent the only living part, the only area invested with personal feeling, the only aspect felt to matter. For no one can their standing among peers be insignificant. A friend alongside, to help, to confide in, the protection of your mates against abuse and warfare, having a laugh, the support and solidarity of your own group – these things must count for pupils at any stage in their school life. By secondary level, particular individuals and encounters may additionally be marked with sexual significance and potentiality. Unlike teacher–pupil relations, those of young people themselves extend into life outside school, and are rich in shared experience and future possibilities.

What place do pupils' interrelationships have in school? The whole system of schooling at best ignores, at worst actually suppresses the vital network of friendship, allegiance, solidarity among children. For young people training to be teachers, the topic of pupil–pupil relations scarcely arises, unless it features as one aspect of problematic discipline. Where particular teachers concern themselves with children's social relationships they have to work against the grain. And this becomes ever harder as schooling progresses. The primary level offers scope for informal talk between pupils, for joint projects and shared learning. At secondary level, though, education becomes in general more and more individualized, its declared goal is solitary testing by examination. In preparation for this goal, young people must learn, with rather rare exceptions, to operate on their own, to view mutual help as unacceptable copying, even cheating. So well is this lesson usually learned that opportunities for collaborative education, in later secondary years, are often rejected, or dismissed as not real work.

Yet if pupils themselves come, through the schooling system, to draw an early separation between their learning and their social lives, this does not eliminate the unalterably social character of classrooms. Class groupings are typically arranged without reference to friendship patterns; any relationships involved are simply referred to, indiscriminately, as 'the peer group'. But the web of social feeling is likely to be highly complicated. However arbitrarily thrown together, children make their own differentiated, personally significant, mutual constructions. Fear and dislike may feature alongside admiration and affection, loneliness alongside affiliation, exclusion alongside a sense of belonging. For all that the transactions of formal education may totally ignore these relations, they nevertheless inform, in subtle, complex ways, the ways in which children engage themselves in the social arena of the classroom. The very vitality of young people's relationships does, in fact, ensure their continuity amidst even the most daunting school surroundings. Friends, routinely separated in class, still manage by significant looks to communicate across the room. Ways of responding to the teacher carry clear messages for other pupils: their approbation, their disapproval, their lack of interest in the encounter is just as clearly conveyed and understood. Where opportunities arise, however unintended, for enhancing social contact, they are likely to be seized. For all the official rhetoric about option choices, most children choose subjects where they can be with their friends.

There are, of course, many teachers, at the secondary as well as the primary level, who are alive to the existence, and the importance, of pupils' interrelations. So, far from trying to suppress or exclude the social feeling among young people, such teachers often see children's relationships as a rich resource in learning. The work of Douglas Barnes, referred to in Chapter 5, provides vivid testimony of the potential fruitfulness of friendship groups learning together where the material of lessons lends itself to collaboration. In my study of collaborative learning (see Chapter 1, note 3), we worked with four such teachers in two inner-city secondary schools. This study, like those of Douglas Barnes, endorsed the conclusion that the integration of pupils' social relationships with their formal learning can be beneficial in many ways. For one teacher, collaborative modes entailed not just the utilization of existing friendships, but a concern with building up and extending friendliness in the classroom, so that isolated and marginal children could become better integrated.

In one second-year humanities class which we studied there were two working-class girls, Tina and Tracey. Their strong friendship provided a particularly interesting basis for their engagement in lessons – interesting, because the academic abilities and school orientations of the two girls were very different. Yet their collaboration seemed to benefit both of them. While Tracey was clearly helped, Tina, the more able girl, also evidently gained rather than being held back. Her efforts at building bridges to the curriculum and communicating her own ideas acted, apparently, to extend her mastery.

Tina's orientation towards school learning was strikingly confident. She was able to discuss school lessons almost as though she was a teacher herself; she debated the relevance of the curriculum for particular pupil groups, she considered different teaching styles, she examined the choice of school texts and suggested alternatives. . . . While appreciating teachers as persons, Tina did not feel dependent on them to mediate learning; in fact, she expressed resentment of those who constantly taught pupils, instead of letting them get on with the work by themselves. . . .

Her friend Tracey spoke from a very different perspective. She clearly saw her own position towards school learning as that of the less able pupil, and frequently made reference to the experience of being at sea in lessons. Her attitude to teachers was in marked contrast to Tina's. For Tracey, school learning seemed to be highly dependent on teachers. . . . So far from endorsing Tina's expectation of relative equality in teacher–pupil relationships, Tracey mistrusted free-and-easy classrooms, and saw teachers as distant authority figures rather than accessible human beings. . . .

In what we saw of these two girls during the year, Tina's characteristic, often enthusiastic commitment carried her less able friend along, often producing real involvement and her own initiative for Tracey, in work they were doing together. Tina's high morale and her readiness to help her friend did not always overcome Tracey's difficulties; on one occasion, after a long period in which Tina made various practical suggestions and showed Tracey her own work, we saw Tracey abandon the task in despair, crumpling up the work she had done. More often, however, the two girls were to be seen involved, often absorbed, in the work they were doing together, proceeding without reference to the teacher.

The firm friendship of these two girls was clearly based on out-of-school concerns. . . . For both girls, life outside school was clearly more important. Tracey, who found school work so difficult and frustrating, described hard-working pupils as goody-goodies, and clearly felt herself to be incompetent, could easily have experienced alienation in Terry's class (as she did in other lessons). On her side, Tina strongly rejected much of the school curriculum. . . . Since she set supreme importance on her social relationships [Terry's] willingness to make room for her friendship with Tracey was obviously critical. . . .

The fact that [these girls] were able to turn their friendship to such account in Terry's classroom . . . is probably due to the mutual sensitivity of the two friends. . . . It was clear that Tina appreciated Tracey as a friend, and that, towards their clearly unequal academic abilities, she took an unsuperior position, tactfully helping Tracey where this was welcome, but not insisting, or dominating her friend. For Tracey, a sense of being respected was crucial; she expressed some bitterness towards a teacher who had been dismissive. It seems likely that her friend's appreciative attitude and delicate handling of her academic difficulties were the critical factors in enabling her to invest herself, to the extent that she did, in the work of Terry's class (Salmon and Claire, 1984, pp. 132–4).

In the same study, we also focused on a fifth-year group working on a social studies option. Here, collaborative modes of learning – for all the personal commitment of the teacher – were far less productive. Among these older pupils, the use of group talk by the teacher, the encouragement of informality and spontaneity, the affirmation of personal experience and judgement, were treated with a certain reserve. Against the background of many years of traditional schooling, these young people generally viewed collaborative modes as a soft option, an interlude of welcome relief from the 'real' work of school – writing done individually.

One teacher's classroom is not, of course, an island. Where individual teachers seek to foster and extend children's positive interrelationships, they are often likely to be doing so within a context that does not recognize the value in school of its pupils' social lives. The disregard, the suppression, of young people's real mutual relations is institutionalized within our educational system. And, in many cases, this may prove disastrous. For those teachers who approach children, appreciating and respecting their existing social relations, a genuinely personal engagement is possible. Knowing a girl's position in a social network, her construction of herself and others within the context of her social world – this is, perhaps, the royal road to knowing that girl. But conversely, an approach which denies children as social agents in their own right, people with vivid, significant and differentiated relations with others, can only act to set up a polarity. To be construed, as a pupil, in terms that deny your own vital engagements, is to find yourself unrecognized, invalidated. The world of such a teacher's classroom is essentially opposed to your own world. The teacher herself is alien, rather than congenial; those who get on in her class are 'them' rather than 'us'. Your engagement with the teacher, if it is not actually hostile, can be no more than instrumental; genuinely personal involvement would be dangerous. So the teacher remains a remote and stereotyped figure, just as, on her side, the pupil, determined to stay wary, to give no hostages to fortune, remains equally unknown, equally stereotyped.

8   The teaching situation

Just back from two weeks in France with a group of third years, the French teacher sails into the staff room. Although she has taught for many years in this school, this is the first time she has taken the children abroad; previously, the task has always been delegated to a younger colleague. To her colleagues, she looks a different person. Previously tired, careworn, harassed, she now steps lightly, holds herself erect; there is a new freedom in all her movements. This woman who is always too preoccupied, too burdened for anything more than the most urgent business, now positively bubbles over with enthusiasm. The rough sea crossing which made such an unpropitious start to the trip; how, along with most of the children, she was terribly sick, and had to defer the activities planned for the rest of the day. Her worries about the shyest, most isolated member of the group, and her surprised relief at the way some of the others had taken her under their wing. The evening sing-songs they had at the hostel, and how well that broke the ice among the various groups there, as well as bridging some of the linguistic gulfs. How returning one afternoon from a museum she had lost the way, and how, to her delighted astonishment, it was the most reluctant speaker of all who risked his French to question a passer-by. Above all, how mature and responsible the group had been throughout the whole trip, showing none of the objectionable behaviour they were capable of in the classroom.

As this teacher announces to her colleagues – listening with weary envy to her unwonted exuberance – her own relationship with these pupils has been altogether transformed. Having got to know each other as individuals, there is a sense of mutual interest, liking and trust. Relations are now personal and intimate, rather than formal or authoritarian. It is impossible for them to revert to the way they were before.

For a few days, these confident anticipations seem to be borne out. The third-year pupils dwell on, mull over their experience with an equal enthusiasm and fascination.. Like their teacher, they remark, wonderingly, on the transformation of their relationship. How different Miss was, she was really human, really nice. It was good to talk to her, she listened to you, she was interested. She wasn't like a teacher at all, she was just a person. For a little while, these feelings, on both sides, give an altogether different character to French lessons. But gradually, another, more familiar atmosphere comes to dominate them – an atmosphere in which, in different ways, both teacher and pupils feel constrained, coerced. Neither side in the classroom relationship has wanted this to happen. Yet neither has been able to stop the gradual deterioration in their relations. Somehow it has proved impossible to sustain, within the classroom, the mutual stance which each took up towards the other in the world beyond.

As social contexts, school classrooms are, of course, very different from those involved in accompanying children on a school trip. For nearly every teacher, the classroom context is one of heavy and multiple pressures. Often these are crystallized as 'the sense of a constant pressure on *time*. This pressure operates at every level. The difficult fifth-year group is, at last, getting interested and involved in the Pinter play they are working on. Yet tomorrow you must leave that, begin a different text, keep up the relentless pace imposed by the exam syllabus. In another class, one child is obviously deeply troubled. But there is no time to talk to him individually, quietly and at length. You can only refer him to the school counsellor, and in the meantime cope as best as you can with the disruptive behaviour through which he regularly expresses his distress. As a teacher you must, of course, keep up with the new developments in your field. It is not just a question of new texts and materials which have somehow to be assimilated. There are also radically different directions to be implemented. The new Local Education Authority initiative, incorporated as a whole school policy, demands a close examination of your teaching for possible sexist biases. To take this seriously seems to call for a sabbatical term at the very least. Yet that is out of the question. Your evenings and free periods are hardly sufficient for marking and preparation: tomorrow's lessons must, after all, take priority. There is only one possibility: your summer holiday, that last reserve of badly needed family time, must be devoted instead to a thorough revision of your teaching.

For most teachers, the pressures felt to operate are not only those of time; there are also social demands which press on them and hem them in. Of all kinds of work, it is teaching, perhaps, which is subject to the most numerous, the most clamorous pressures from other groupings. It is probable that in no other work situation do so many different kinds of people feel such a strong and legitimate interest. Parents, employers, politicians, the community at large, special interest groups all have their vital investment in schooling. More formally, the universities and training institutions, the educational establishment, the LEAs and their advisers make their own authoritative demands on classroom business. And more closely still, the influence of head teachers, heads of department, senior colleagues, is felt, keenly if implicitly, by most teachers as they conduct their individual work. For all that classrooms are ostensibly private places, where single teachers have their own, unseen dealings with the children in their class, in practice most teachers bring with them a whole host of voices, making loud, conflicting demands. If those who teach often express a sense of being beleaguered, this does not really seem surprising.

Nor is it only adult groupings which, formally or informally, press their demands upon teachers. Lively, active children and young people, who must spend their time as pupils in school, do not merely wait passively for what is to happen there. They bring their own wills and expectations – their hopes and interests, or, conversely, their resentment, frustration, boredom, restlessness. The transactions, the activities of the classroom are, obviously, not just the creation of the teacher, but a product of the constant and active negotiation between the often conflicting desires and intentions of teacher and pupils. For many a teacher, the intensity of these moment-to-moment pressures – the sheer difficulty of staying in control of events, keeping one step ahead of twenty-five restless, ebullient young people – creates a sense of non-manoeuvrability, of having no breathing space. So far from feeling in charge of every initiative, many teachers define their task as one of just trying to respond adequately to those of their pupils. They may see themselves, however regretfully, as essentially reactive rather than proactive in their work. One aspect of this situation is the seeming impossibility of change. Though you know that your handling of some regularly recurring problems is less than satisfactory, under the pressure of the moment you cannot help falling back into the old reactions.

Subjected daily to all these kinds of pressure, most people in the teaching profession are liable, at times, to feel a sense of fragmentation, perhaps even of alienation. The focus of multiple, often irreconcilable demands, their work may seem to get pushed and pulled in all sorts of contradictory directions. Nominally in charge of things, they may feel their real power as teachers to be a hollow one. At moments such as these, the men and women involved are apt to experience a personal separation between themselves and their work. As individuals, they cannot identify with their teaching role, which remains merely a part they are playing – a part which has little resonance in their deepest feelings, their most significant hopes and intentions. In this situation, teachers hear in their daily classroom work a whole chorus of loudly demanding voices: the one voice they cannot hear is their own.

Yet for everyone who teaches, their situation is unique. Despite the apparent uniformity of many teachers' positions, each person constructs their own version of classroom reality, its meanings for their work, its constraints and possibilities. In an unusual, highly personal study, Anthony Rosie (1979) closely examined the subjective positions of three teachers in the English department of an outer London comprehensive. Himself a member of the same department, Rosie had established a remarkable level of trust on the part of his colleagues, who spoke to him very openly of their experience. For all three teachers the situation is extremely delicate and fraught with difficulty.

Here is Rosie's sketch of the three teachers involved:

Jeff. Jeff was now the new Head of Department. Aged 32, he had taught in a number of schools and was keen to develop mixed-ability teaching and a language policy as it was envisaged in the Bullock Report (1975).

Stephen. Stephen was in charge of the internal examinations and some of the public examinations. Aged 47, he had taught at the school for ten years having taught in a variety of other schools.

Jean. Jean was in charge of Drama teaching. Aged 33, she had taught at the school for four years after training as a mature student. This was the only school where she had taught (Rosie, 1979, pp. 328–9).

During the year in which Jeff has been head of department, both Stephen and Jean have come to see his position as polarized in relation to their own. So impossible does the situation seem to both of them, that each is contemplating resignation. Stephen remarks, 'Well, I will probably leave when my wife finishes the course she is doing. I need the money and I've been a Head of Department before and I've done all the work.' And Jean comments, 'I think I will leave. I wish I had stuck to my guns before when I handed in my notice.' What kind of construction has led to such drastic solutions on the part of these two teachers?

In his analysis, Rosie begins by looking at all three teachers' views of a number of dimensions relating to pupil behaviour. As part of an examination of the school curriculum, all the teachers have completed a questionnaire in which they endorse or question the importance of a number of dimensions:

> Being quiet and orderly
> Not interrupting the teacher when he or she is speaking
> Wearing school uniform
> Doing homework
> Paying attention in class
> Keeping up with the work
> Learning to work on your own.

In their responses, both Stephen and Jean express strong agreement that all these dimensions are important for pupils, whereas Jeff feels that other dimensions, notably promoting conversation in class, are equally important. These differences in emphasis become more evident when Rosie invites the three teachers to consider the dimensions from another angle.

Each teacher is asked to define, for each dimension, what they see as its contrast; then, considering this contrast, to define what would be *its* essential contrast. This rather oblique operation produces a more personal rendering of the original officially labelled dimensions. In the case of four dimensions, Stephen and Jean offer definitions which are clearly different from those of Jeff.

Original	Stephen	Jean	Jeff
Not interrupting the teacher	Being courteous	Being well behaved	Being interested in the lesson
Paying attention in class	Getting on with the work	Getting on with the work	Feel it necessary to listen to the teacher
Keeping up with the work	Capable of doing the work	Able to do the work without trouble	Finding the work interesting
Learning to work on your own	Working on your own	Becoming independent	Discovering that teachers don't know anything

These alternative slants on the same starting point illustrate two very different kinds of teaching orientations. On their side, Stephen and Jean speak from positions close to that of the original list of dimensions – emphasizing the importance of order in the classroom, of quietness and good behaviour, of attention to teacher instruction. For Jeff, on the other hand, recognition of pupil subjectivity is vital; he speaks from a position which affirms the importance of children's active engagement in classroom work. Such differences do indeed seem profound.

On this evidence, Jean and Stephen share closely similar positions. Yet, as Rosie illustrates, they are in fact quite diverse. Though both emphasize good behaviour, for Jean this feature has meaning, ultimately, in terms of caring and supportive relationships. It is from this viewpoint, too, that she defines her present situation as intolerable.

No one seems to spend time on people here and there's no caring. It's the little things that matter. . . . I don't like the way the department is going. We are never told anything and there seems to be no clear direction. . . . At first I thought [Jeff] was a welcome change. He was interested in Drama and he wanted to do things. But then we got nowhere. He never remembered what it was like for me to teach eight periods of Drama a day (Rosie, 1979, p. 333).

For Stephen, good behaviour on the part of pupils is also crucial, but this carries rather different connotations.

> I insist on order in the classroom and I won't have children disobeying me. They must learn that I'm in authority (ibid., p. 332).

Stephen views teaching as establishing status 'which confers duties and powers'; it is the teacher's responsibility, and right, to demand proper order from his pupils. This responsibility also extends into making important judgements about pupils' ability levels and their progress – judgements which should not be passed over or called into question. It is in this sphere that, for Stephen, his relations with Jeff are felt to be most problematic.

> I don't see how Jeff and I can get on. He believes in mixed–ability but of course it doesn't work. I don't agree with his ideas. To be honest with you, they aren't liked by parents or teachers in junior schools. Take this new business of not marking every mistake and not giving a numerical mark for younger children. It annoys me. It goes against everything I believe in (ibid., p. 334).

How does Jeff see things? He is well aware that there are serious problems in his department.

> I know there's a rift between Stephen, Jean and myself. For Stephen I think the fact that he is the oldest person in the department and has always believed in rules has formed his outlook. He is not sympathetic to the needs of children. He works hard according to his lights but its lists and rules, no thinking (ibid., p. 335).

Evidently, between Stephen and Jeff little real sociality exists. Stephen rejects Jeff's approach out of hand. 'Of course it doesn't work', 'I don't agree with his ideas', 'It goes against everything I believe in.' Jeff's construction of Stephen is not quite so dismissive. He acknowledges the high value which Stephen puts on status, and recognizes that many years of teaching according to rules has made it difficult for him to be flexible. Yet this understanding is not an appreciative one: 'He is not sympathetic to the needs of children', 'It's all lists and rules, no thinking.'

As far as relations between Jean and Jeff are concerned, things seem to be even worse. On her side, Jean views Jeff as essentially uncaring: 'not spending time with people', 'failing in little things', 'never remembering what it's like to teach eight periods of Drama a day'. In his perspective on Jean, Jeff shows no awareness of her distress in feeling unsupported in her work. Instead, he defines her as an essentially problematic person, whose difficulties lie outside the school context:

I think Jean needs help. She is obviously under strain but she doesn't respond too well. I don't think her problems are necessarily school-based but she is beginning to cause trouble (Rosie, 1979, p. 335).

This case study shows three teachers badly at odds with each other. For each of them, the positions of their colleagues are critically important. No classroom is an island. Teachers, in their individual dealings with pupils, are apt to be keenly aware of support or challenge from those around them. Where a teacher's own approach is at variance with that of the school, the head or head of department, her classroom is permeated, invaded, by another frame of reference – alien, hostile, threatening. The drastic solution of resigning, contemplated by both Stephen and Jean, would, in such a situation, not really be surprising.

Fortunately, such extreme dissension among close colleagues is not the norm. However, most teachers probably experience, if not actual hostility, a sense of isolation and lack of support from all but a few of their teaching colleagues. In Kellyan terms, the situation of teachers is typically one in which sociality is not easily developed. For all the numerous meetings – departmental, house, whole school, with parents, formal or informal, regular or crisis – there are likely to be few occasions on which it is possible to talk together openly, freely, and at length. Within the narrow constraints imposed by institutional expectations of proper teaching behaviour, there is little freedom for the expression of real feelings. The consciousness of a private departure in one's own teaching from normative practice, or of failure in a beginning teacher to maintain 'proper order' in the classroom, makes it necessary for particular people to keep a low profile. For everybody, there is likely to be a conspiracy of silence on the topic of personal doubts and difficulties in teaching. If staff room cultures allow certain pupils, or groups of pupils, to be defined as deviant, objectionable, problematic, they absolutely forbid the confession of your own sense of failure, conflict or despair. The presence of others higher in the school hierarchy – people who could block your promotion prospects – represents a threat to free expression, and makes for personal guardedness rather than a genuine sharing of experience.

A major aspect of this situation is that it limits teachers' awareness of their own positions. Without the opportunity to articulate some of the basic assumptions from which we act, we cannot begin to reflect upon the meaning of the work we do. This reflection is particularly vital when things are going badly. Unless we can consider the situation in depth, see what is essentially involved, at stake, and envisage whether there might be other avenues of approach, we cannot escape the same old vicious circle. Faced, for the umpteenth time, with the growing uproar of a bored and restless class on a sweltering Friday afternoon, you find yourself yet again shouting at them. You can hear yourself beginning to lose your self-control, you know the children can sense it too. This is no way to restore calm and sanity; it can only produce an escalation of disorder and violence. But you are dog-tired at the end of a heavy week, it is only three weeks into the term, and you have a full schedule of marking and preparation filling the weekend ahead. You must at all costs stop this unruly, uproarious behaviour; what else *is* there to do?

Routine teaching situations rarely present the opportunity to reflect on the personal assumptions that underlie teaching practices. But, in a growing number of school contexts, some teachers are beginning to create such opportunities for themselves. Occasionally this is an individual effort. Lee Enright (1979), for instance, decided to submit her own teaching to careful scrutiny and reflection. She kept a diary of each day's work and tape-recorded some of her own lessons. She also talked to her pupils about the work she was doing with them. As she describes, this exercise proved very illuminating. After a year, she found herself much more closely aware of her pupils' reactions and perceptions; her role towards them seemed, concomitantly, to have altered in ways which greatly reduced previous problems of discipline.

For most people, it is difficult, entirely alone, to become aware of the basis from which you act, and to begin to question and elaborate it. All this is much easier if you can work together with someone else. One of the people who has pioneered this kind of collaborative partnership is Michael Armstrong (1986). In order to explore and take further his own experience as a junior school teacher, Armstrong arranged to work for a year as a supplementary teacher in the classroom of a colleague, Stephen Rowland. At the end of each day, Armstrong wrote up, over two or three hours, a full account of his experience of the day's classroom events. Shared with Rowland, these accounts proved highly fruitful in shaping both observation and practice, and in defining further inquiry into how children develop intellectually in classroom settings.

On a still broader basis, some teachers manage to form their own research groups, often spanning a wide variety of settings. As Josie Levine (1986), convenor of one such group, describes, the helpfulness of this context derives both from its diversity and from its constructive, mutually supportive character:

The Teachers' Research Group is a forum where teachers can discuss their practice, implement some sort of investigation into it, develop ideas and understanding about it. . . . It provides teachers with the welcome opportunity of working with others not only from schools and authorities outside their own, but also across age ranges. Often, through this, they find support and encouragement for thinking and practice they are unable to find at home. Equally people are in a position to learn from educational developments and practices in age ranges other than the ones in which they themselves may be working. All of which adds up to a practice which affords a useful co-ordination of insights which would not otherwise be available (p. 16).

Yet, even given the expertise and support of such ongoing groups as this, actually changing one's own practice remains a personally difficult act. It is one thing to learn of a colleague's successful approach to a shared problem, but quite another to take that approach on board yourself. We all act out of a sense of our own personal identity. What we do, how we behave, how we relate to others has to square with this fundamental identity if we are to maintain a feeling of integrity. Our identity is, besides, lodged not only privately within ourselves. It has been built up through our dealings with other people; it is jointly constituted, and has its reality in their experience too.

One evening, in your teachers' research group, you are discussing the problem of second language speakers, a problem which, as you are all too well aware, you have not even begun to resolve. A fellow teacher describes with enthusiastic conviction how he approaches things: enlisting parents to translate worksheets, bringing in visiting second language speakers, setting up games in which indigenous children have to learn from their ESL classmates. This is working very well for him; why not, as he encouragingly suggests, try this approach yourself? You can only agree that these strategies might produce an equal breakthrough in your own classroom. Yet somehow, the prospect of actually adopting them is not straightforward. It is all very well for him, but you are not really that sort of teacher. Your dealings with parents and the community have never been casual or informal. Opening up your lessons to people from outside would be a major departure from the teaching approach you have always taken. And what would happen if you were to introduce games into your classroom? Might not things degenerate into a situation you could not control? Nor, it seems, could you even begin to try all this without a loss of general credibility. Wherever you have taught, the children have always seen you as a formal teacher, strict but fair, who takes her classroom work seriously. To your colleagues, too, you are known as someone who stands for traditional values, who insists, in her teaching, on the fundamental importance of order, respect, authority.

Personal change is never easy. For teachers, in particular, the construction of viable alternatives – other ways of doing things which seem personally consonant and valid – is likely to be especially problematic. Beleaguered, embattled, hemmed in, teachers must fight hard even to maintain things as they are, let alone find the breathing space to try out other, personally risky alternatives. But if daily classroom work leaves most people little room for manoeuvre, in-service education can, perhaps, provide its own opportunities. It is in this sphere that the pioneering work of an Australian psychologist, Patrick Diamond (1982a and b, 1985), suggests exciting possibilities.

Diamond's approach to in-service teacher education is founded in the recognition that teachers, while often dissatisfied with their own work, nevertheless tend to feel trapped, unable to create other ways of doing things:

Teaching can be depicted as a process which almost inevitably involves paradox and dilemma since most of the research strongly confirms the existence of inconsistencies between what the teacher

wants to do and what they actually do. . . . It is quite erroneous
to assume substantial implementation of teachers' own ideas versus
preferred practices. As teachers go busily about their daily chores,
the disparity is enormous (1982b, p. 31).

For most teachers, this situation comes to be experienced as
one of personal helplessness:

Teachers themselves agree that this kind of second best accords with
their experience and that too little of what they want ever seems
to eventuate. The usual explanation is that 'They won't let me'!
where the interfering 'they' takes the form of the education system
and its officers, the local school administration and even the current
student body. . . . Instead of blaming themselves for the
discrepancy and the frustration, teachers can safely see themselves
as thwarted persons capable of great things if only they were
allowed to do so (1982b, p. 31).

In keeping with the tough tone of these remarks, Diamond sets
out in his work to challenge this sense of personal helplessness.
In this he follows closely Kelly's own most radical approach
to the problem of personal change – the use of fixed role
therapy.

As a therapist, Kelly was concerned with the traps his clients
often built for themselves by thinking in pre-emptive rather
than propositional terms. Pre-emptive thinking sets things in
concrete, allowing no alternative possibilities. As a woman, I
must defer to men, I must be sensitive to the feelings of those
around me, I must support other people and not expect them
to support me. If you think in these terms, you have little
freedom of manoeuvre. Change can only be slot change, that
is, a complete reversal of your usual behaviour – something
likely to be quite disturbing both to others and to yourself.
But suppose you consider yourself in propositional rather than
pre-emptive terms. If, as a woman, I were to take up car
maintenance, extend my understanding of that interesting but
unfamiliar sphere, what would it be like? Into what new realms
of experience might the learning lead me, and how might that
enhance and elaborate my womanliness? In Kelly's terms, this is
to use the invitational mode: to think in tentative, hypothetical
ways, to try things out provisionally. The changes involved in
provisional thinking are not simply a reversal of our usual
assumptions; instead, they entail fundamental shifts in the

dimensions that give meaning to our experience. This kind of construing means suspending, for the time being, our habitual hard and fast positions in the realization that there can be no single, final way of defining our lives.

Fixed role therapy was the procedure whereby Kelly set out to facilitate provisional thinking in his clients, and to support them while, for a short period, they tried out, personally enacted, an alternative construction of their situation. Essentially, the procedure entails devising a possible perspective on things, built upon the client's existing perspective but giving it a new slant. The client then, for a fixed period, attempts actually to live according to this perspective. During this trial period, the adviser offers regular consultation and support.

In using this procedure with teachers on an in-service education course, Diamond begins by inviting participants to produce a sketch of themselves as particular teachers. Since he has worked mainly with teachers of composition (written English), it is to that curriculum area that his account refers.

By examining the sketch, the teacher educator may see how their construct systems have enabled them to paint themselves into a corner with virtually no way out. . . . The teacher educator draws up a portrait of another teacher who is ninety degrees to the original teacher's pedagogical self-portrait. . . . For example, if he or she has taught skills in isolation, he or she is asked to teach them in context. The problem is to help the teacher find new dimensions along which to see the teaching of composition and not merely to slot rattle, for example, from 'slave to patrician', 'from incompetent to superstar' or from 'teaching to non-interference. . . .

The created role character is shown to the teacher, who is asked if such a teacher is credible and even likeable. If not it is altered until it is. The teacher is then asked to 'be' the fictitious teacher for, say, the next three weeks in the classroom. The teacher is to set the kind of writing assignments he or she thinks such a teacher would devise, to do that teacher's kinds of personal writing, to read those kinds of books and articles, to respond to students' questions and written productions and seek to interpret lessons entirely in terms of this 'fictional' teacher.

This may sound like an impossible undertaking, but its express limits make it easier for teachers to try it.

It is emphasized that this is only a limited venture and at the conclusion of the time the teacher is to revert to his or her own teaching identity. The new role is not an ideal but merely an hypothesis – an invitation to conjecture . . . the alternative sketch enables teachers to explore tentatively the possibilities of other approaches to teaching. When the teachers realise that what is being tested is only a hypothesis, they can begin to feel more comfortable investing their efforts in something less than the whole of their personal and professional lives (1982a, p. 170).

The purpose of this personal experiment – during which there are regular tutorial consultations – is to provide an experience of the fact that alternative approaches are always available.

Many teachers of composition may be endlessly and futilely drilling the skills in isolation simply because no alternative has ever been suggested in a way that makes personal sense. Before they can begin to teach for communicative growth or personal fulfilment, teaching the skills in context has to become meaningful to them. The fixed role sketch makes this possible. They learn to concentrate on construing composition from this stance. Most teachers . . . have teaching moments that allow of greater pupil choice and insight. Those experiences can form the basis of change and controlled role elaboration. Each such episode, orchestrated by the fixed role sketch, can be discussed in detail, the teachers being helped to construe as much as possible about it, including unintended results. Very often the teachers have not done this after something new (such as pupils offering to share their own poems) has worked. They have construed it globally as just different. They have not looked to see what was different in how they felt and behaved, how the pupils reacted and what aspects of the classroom might have led to their being, for example, more child-oriented and less grammar-centred (1982a, pp. 170–1).

Through their engagement in these personally adventurous experiments, the teachers on Diamond's in-service training courses typically find an enlargement of their professional horizons. Before the role enactment, for instance, one teacher described herself as 'often frustrated by the fact that neither she nor her students lived up to the ideals she had for them all'. After this period, she stated that her single priority had become to challenge her students, to stimulate them to explore themselves and their world.

Having undertaken, for a trial period, a new kind of stance towards their work, these teachers find that things are far less fixed than they had come to believe. There are, it seems, choices, alternatives, possibilities in their teaching situation:

> If they began by seeking refuge, excusing themselves as pawns having little impact, they may in fact conclude by seeing themselves as capable of leading and inspiring their classes. . . . If the programmes have been successful, the teachers will view the changes as largely their own achievements and realise that it is only the beginning (1985, p. 171).

Alas, developmental opportunities like these are all too rare, even for those seconded to in-service training courses. Most practising teachers inhabit contexts that are a world away from these supported experimental ventures. Yet Diamond's work shows that, in the end, Kelly was right. The personal reality of the situations in which we work is one which, together with others, we ourselves have created. Merely realizing this does not, of itself, allow any easy solution. Nor, usually, can individual efforts get very far. Only on the margins of official school life can corners sometimes be found, or spaces made, where teachers can talk together freely, honestly, without defensiveness or competition. There, in an atmosphere of shared concern and thoughtful, imaginative exploration, it may sometimes be possible jointly to reconstruct the social engagements of teaching.

Notes

Introduction

1   Kelly's lengthy book, *The Psychology of Personal Constructs* (Norton 1955), formally presents his theoretical system. The first volume contains a detailed exposition of the theory, presented as a fundamental postulate with eleven corollaries. The second volume illustrates the theory by reference to clinical applications.

   Because of its highly formal presentation, and academic, sometimes abstruse language, this book has remained closed to all but a few dedicated readers. Most people who have read about the approach have done so via the much more accessible introduction written by Don Bannister and Fay Fransella, *Inquiring Man: The Psychology of Personal Constructs* (3rd edn, 1986 Croom Helm). This paperback book has been hugely successful and is now in a third edition.

   However, following his original exposition, Kelly himself evidently felt free to express his ideas in much less formal ways. A number of his essays, papers and conference addresses were gathered together, after his death in 1966, by Brendan Maher, as *Clinical Psychology and Personality: The Papers of George Kelly* (Robert E. Krieger Pub. Co. 1979). Eloquent, funny, personal, this book, beyond all others, probably best conveys the human character of Kellyan psychology.

2   This change in nomenclature reflects the general consensus that what Kelly offered was not so much a theory as such, but rather a certain approach to psychology, a distinctive way of looking at human life.

3   Don Bannister built his work on the rationale that schizophrenic thought disorder is the outcome of repeatedly experiencing invalidation of crucial constructs about oneself in relation to others. The logic of this rationale was tested, and confirmed, in a number of key experiments. First, Bannister showed that thought disorder, alone among psychiatric conditions, entails a loss of conceptual structure in the area of psychological construing. This lack of structure, as he next showed, is specific to the psychological sphere, and does not apply to other areas of construing. Finally, by experimentally manipulating validational evidence,

Bannister demonstrated that loss of conceptual structure, in psychological construing, is contingent upon the experience of repeated invalidation.

This work is described briefly in Bannister and Fransella, *Inquiring Man: The Psychology of Personal Constructs* (3rd edn, Fontana). A more detailed account is given in Bannister's journal articles, listed in the References, from 1962 to 1966.

4 Laurie Thomas has worked over many years, with colleagues at the Centre for Human Learning, Brunel University, to apply Kelly's ideas to the area of learning and education. His research has been informed by a concern to put learning in the charge of learners themselves, by facilitating self-organization, learning to learn, and learner-based modes of instruction. Thomas's main instruments, in this research, have been developments of Kelly's repertory grid technique. This technique, which is based on a sorting task, is essentially an invitation to subjects to try out and make explicit their own personal construing. With the help of computer-based analyses, subjects can then develop their construing further. Thomas's work is described in Thomas, L. and Harri-Augstein, E. S. (1985), *Self-organized Learning: Foundations of a Conversational Science for Psychology*, Routledge and Kegan Paul.

5 Together with Terence Keen, Maureen Pope offers a useful summary of Kellyan research in the field of education, in Pope, M. and Keen, T. (1981), *Personal Construct Psychology and Education*, Academic Press.

Chapter 1 *A Kellyan approach*

1 The two rather different techniques of assessment which Kelly devised nevertheless stem from the same first principle – the primacy of first-person statements. Repertory grid technique, which has been widely used (and often misused), is a method of assessing, in mathematical terms, the interrelationship between a sample of the subject's personal constructs. For a full account of this technique, see Fransella and Bannister, 1977. The second technique, self-characterization, is essentially qualitative rather than quantitative. Subjects are invited to write a character sketch of themselves. This is taken to convey something of the way they see themselves in relation to their own worlds. For a brief discussion and illustration of this technique, see Bannister and Fransella, 1986.

2 See previous note.

3 In this SSRC-funded research project I worked, jointly with an ex-teacher, to explore collaborative modes of learning in two inner-city comprehensives. The study was framed within Kellyan

ideas, and viewed classroom collaboration as entailing commonality (common ground) and sociality (mutual understanding), both
among pupils and between pupils and teachers. We worked with
four teachers – of social studies (fifth year), design and technology,
drama and history (all second year). In each classroom, we took
the teacher's frame of reference to define and evaluate the learning
there. Broadly, the outcomes of the work were encouraging, and
showed that social relationships between pupils could provide the
basis of learning, rather than merely representing a source of
disruption.

4 Personal communication. In his own sphere as an educational
psychologist, Ravenette has developed personal construct
psychology in inventive and illuminating ways. Unfortunately,
little of his work is generally available. In one recent paper,
however, Ravenette makes some interesting suggestions about
referrals to educational psychologists:

> Personal construct psychology leads to an insistence on taking the teacher
> aspect of referral very seriously. The psychologist needs not only to look
> where the teacher's finger points, but to the teacher behind the finger
> and the constructs which lie behind the teacher. In effect we ask of the
> teacher 'What is the problem for which the referral is a solution?' recog-
> nizing that behind the obvious answer i.e. the complaint, there is an
> unverbalized, because unrecognized, answer which is personal to the
> teacher (Ravenette, A. T. (1987), 'Personal construct psychology in the
> practice of an educational psychologist', in G. Dunnett (ed.), *Personal
> Construct Psychology in Clinical Settings*, in press, Routledge & Kegan
> Paul).

5 In Kelly's terms 'Hostility is the continued effort to extort validational evidence in favour of a type of social prediction which has
already been recognised as a failure.' This definition distinguishes
hostility from aggression; in fact hostile behaviour – as a strategy
which attempts to preserve the person from the need for massive
reconstruing – may take many forms.

6 In Kelly's terms, 'Anxiety is awareness that the events with which
one is confronted lie mostly outside the range of convenience of
one's construct system.' In this definition, it is the unknown
implications of a situation – the fact that we can only partially
construe it – which make for anxious feelings.

7 In a startling comparison, Kelly declared that the quest of a
research student and a psychotherapy client were essentially the
same. Both faced the same difficult sequence of tasks: to pinpoint
crucial issues, put them to critical test, honestly evaluate the
evidence, and revise their thinking to accommodate what they
had learned.

Chapter 4   *Personal education*

1   Mrs Mary Warnock chaired a committee of inquiry, set up by the government, into the education of handicapped children and young people. The committee produced its influential report in 1979. It advised that at any one time, one child in every six attending school was likely to need help. The committee recommended that the statutory categories of handicap be abolished, reference being made instead to special educational needs. A central principle in the report was the desirability of integrating children with special needs into ordinary schools.

Chapter 5   *The process of learning*

1   Kelly saw change and stability in construing as contingent upon validational fortunes. Validation of our anticipations acts to confirm our construing, while invalidation disconfirms it and leads to some kind of change or reconstruction. It is in this sphere that the work of Don Bannister, on schizophrenic thought disorder, has both supported and developed Kelly's ideas.

Chapter 6   *The substrate of schooling*

1   The committee chaired by David Hargreaves was set up by the Inner London Education Authority to inquire into the curriculum and organization of its secondary schools. Its report, *Improving Secondary Schools*, which appeared in 1984, recommended a considerable enlargement of the traditional secondary curriculum. This included the recommendation that all fourth and fifth year pupils should take compulsory courses in personal and social education.

2   See Chapter 1, note 3, for an outline of Don Bannister's work.

3   The Humanities Curriculum Project (1970) was funded jointly by the Schools Council and the Nuffield Foundation. Lawrence Stenhouse has summarized the project as follows:

'The Humanities Project – of which I was director – was like most patterns of action research in education, complex and multi-faceted. Its occasion was the raising of the school-leaving age and its justification in political terms (for policy and pedagogy must both be satisfied in education) was seen in the possibility of its offering an ethical basis for the accountability of teachers to pupils, parents and society for their handling of contentious controversial issues in the classroom. Its definition of content was "controversial human issues of universal concern" ' (Stenhouse, Verman, Wild and Nixon 1984, p. 5).

References

Armstrong, M. (1986), 'Thinking about children's learning: Reflections on an enquiry', *Forum*, **29** no. 1, pp. 11–13.

Ashton-Warner, S. (1963), *Teacher*, Secker & Warburg

Bannister, D. (1962), 'The nature and measurement of schizophrenic thought disorder', *Journal of Mental Science*, **108**, pp. 825–42

Bannister, D. (1963), 'The genesis of schizophrenic thought disorder: A serial invalidation hypothesis', *British Journal of Psychiatry*, **109**, pp. 680–9

Bannister, D. (1965), 'The genesis of schizophrenic thought disorder: Re-test of the serial invalidation hypothesis', *British Journal of Psychiatry*, **111**, pp. 377–82

Bannister, D. and Fransella, F. (1986), *Inquiring Man: The Psychology of Personal Constructs* (3rd edn, Croom Helm)

Bannister, D. and Salmon, P. (1966), 'Schizophrenic thought disorder: Specific or diffuse?' *British Journal of Medical Psychology*, **39**, pp. 215–19

Barnes, D., Britton, J. and Torbe, M. (1986), *Language, the Learner & the School*, Penguin (Torbe, M. 'Language across the curriculum: Policies and practice'; Barnes, D., 'Language in the secondary classroom')

Baur, M. C. (1981), 'Social interaction in primary school classrooms, and the perceptions and experiences of teachers and pupils', Unpublished Ph.D thesis, University of London

Berger, P. L. and Luckmann, T. (1967), *The Social Construction of Reality*, Doubleday

Bernstein, B. (1971), 'On the classification and framing of educational knowledge', in M. F. D. Young (ed.), *Knowledge and Control*, Collier-Macmillan

Bernstein, B. (1982), 'Codes, modalities and the process of cultural reproduction: A model', in M. Apple (ed.), *Cultural and Economic Reproduction in Education*, Routledge & Kegan Paul

Blishen, E. (1969), *The School that I'd Like*, Penguin Education

Brierley, D. W. (1967), 'The use of personality constructions by children of three different ages', Unpublished Ph.D thesis, University of London

Brittain, E. M. (1976), 'Multi-racial education', *Educational Research*, **18**, pp. 3–20.

Brophy, J. and Good, T. (1974), *Teacher–Student Relationships: Causes and Consequences*, Holt Rinehart & Winston

Broverman, I., Broverman, D., Clarkson, F., Rosenkrantz, P. and Vogel, S. (1970), 'Sex role stereotypes and clinical judgements of mental health', *Journal of Consulting & Clinical Psychology*, **34**, pp. 1–7

Commission for Racial Equality (1985), *Birmingham Local Education Authority: Referral and Suspension of Pupils*, Commission for Racial Equality

Diamond, C. T. P. (1982a), 'Teachers can change: A Kellyan interpretation', *Journal of Education for Teaching*, **8** no. 2, pp. 162–72

Diamond, C. T. P. (1982b), 'You always end up with conflict: An account of constraints in teaching written composition', in R. E. Eagleson (ed.), *English in the Eighties*, Sydney: AATE

Diamond, C. T. P. (1985), 'Fixed role treatment: Creating alternative scenarios', *Australian Journal of Education*, **29**, pp. 161–73

Donaldson, M. (1978), *Children's Minds*, Fontana

Driver, C. (1981), 'Classroom stress and school achievement: West Indian adolescents and their teachers', in A. James and R. Jeffcoate (eds.), *The School in the Multi-Cultural Society*, Harper & Row

Egan, K. (1986), *Individual Development and the Curriculum*, Hutchinson

Emler, N. and Heather, N. (1980), 'Intelligence: An ideological bias of conventional psychology', in P. Salmon (ed.), *Coming to Know*, Routledge & Kegan Paul

Enright, L. (1976), 'Learning in my classroom', *Forum*, **21** no. 3, pp. 78–81

Fransella, F. and Bannister, D. (1977), *A Manual for Repertory Grid Technique*, Academic Press

Humanities Curriculum Project (1970), *The Humanities Project: An Introduction*, Heinemann Educational

Jackson, B. (1979), *Starting School*, Croom Helm

Jahoda, G. (1983), 'European "lag" in the development of an economic concept: A study in Zimbabwe', *British Journal of Developmental Psychology*, **1**, pp. 113–20

Kelly G. A. (1955), *The Psychology of Personal Constructs*, Norton

Kelly, G. A. (1979a), 'Hostility', in B. Maher (ed.), *Clinical Psychology and Personality: The Selected Papers of George Kelly*, Rober Krieger Pub. Co.

Kelly, G. A. (1979b), 'Sin and psychotherapy', in B. Maher (ed.), *Clinical Psychology and Personality: The Selected Papers of George Kelly*, Robert Krieger Pub. Co.

Kohl, H. (1971), *36 Children*, Penguin

Lee, L. (1965), *Cider with Rosie*, Hogarth Press

Levine, J. (1986), 'A teachers' research group', *Forum*, **29**, pp. 16–18

Morrison, A. and McIntyre, D. (eds.) (1972), *The Social Psychology of Teaching*, Penguin Education

Newell, P. (1983), 'Strategies for integration', in A. Shearer (ed.), *Integration: A New Partnership?*, Advisory Centre for Education and The Spastics Society

Phillips, E. M. (1982), 'Developing by design', *Vocational Aspects of Education*, **34**, pp. 31–6

Piaget, J. (1958), *The Child's Construction of Reality*, Routledge & Kegan Paul

Pope, M. and Keen, T. (1981), *Personal Construct Theory and Education*, Academic Press

Postman, N. and Weingartner, C. (1969), *Teaching as a Subversive Activity*, Penguin Education

Potts, P. (1984), 'Integrating pre-school with special needs', Centre for Studies on Integration in Education

Powell, J. L. (1985), *The Teacher's Craft*, Scottish Council for Research in Education

Rogers, C. (1983), *Freedom to learn for the 80s*, Charles Merrill Pub. Co.

Rosenthal, R. and Jacobsen, L. (1968), *Pygmalion in the Classroom*, Holt, Rinehart & Winston

Rosie, A. J. (1979), 'Teachers and children: Interpersonal relations in the classroom', in P. Stringer and D. Bannister (eds.), *Constructions of Sociality and Individuality*, Academic Press

Runkel, P. J. and Damrin, D. E. (1961), 'The effect of training and anxiety upon teachers' preferences for information about students', *Educational Psychology*, **52**, pp. 254–61

Salmon, P. and Claire, H. (1984), *Classroom Collaboration*, Routledge & Kegan Paul

Sharp, R. and Green, A. (1976), *Education and Social Control: a study in progressive primary education*, Routledge & Kegan Paul

Stenhouse, L., Verma, G. K., Wild, R. D. J. and Nixon, J. (1984), *Teaching about Race Relations: Problems and Effects*, Routledge & Kegan Paul

Thomas, L. F. and Harri-Augstein, S. (1985), *Self-organized Learning*, Routledge & Kegan Paul

Tizard, B. and Hughes, M. (1984), *Young Children Learning*, Fontana

Walden, R. and Walkerdine, V. (1985), *Girls and Mathematics: from primary to secondary schooling*, University of London Institute of Education

Willes, M. J. (1983), *Children into Pupils*, Routledge & Kegan Paul

Young, R. M., 'Racist society, racist science', *Multicultural Teaching*, **V** no. 3, 1987

Index